Glacier National l

Travel Guide 2025:

Hiking Trails, Wildlife Encounters, and Scenic Wonders

By

Renee A. Gould

Table of content

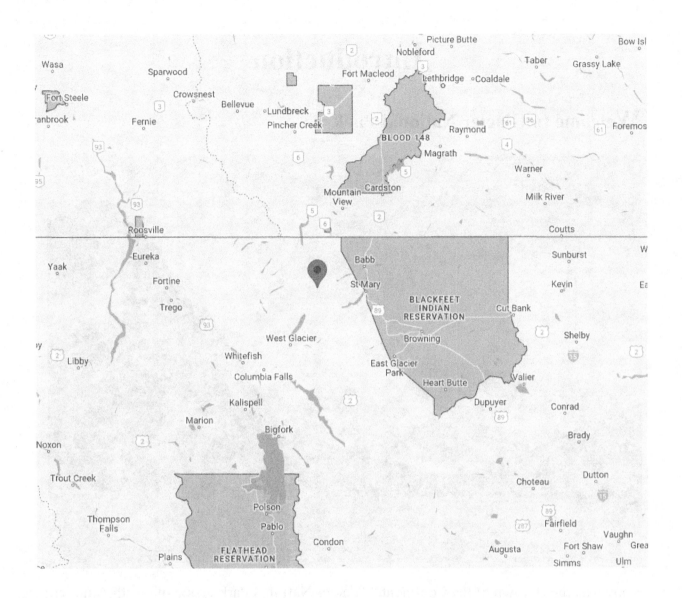

Introduction

Welcome to Glacier National Park

Known as the "Crown of the Continent," Glacier National Park is one of North America's most stunning and untouched natural areas. Located in Montana's northern Rocky Mountains, near the Canadian border, the park is a treasure for nature lovers, adventurers, and anyone seeking to experience the beauty of the natural world. Spanning over a million acres, Glacier National Park is home to rugged mountains, deep valleys, clear lakes, and a diverse array of plant and animal life, offering visitors an extraordinary experience.

Part of the larger Crown of the Continent ecosystem, the park is connected to Canada's Waterton Lakes National Park, forming the Waterton-Glacier International Peace Park, a UNESCO World Heritage Site. This designation highlights the global importance of the area's natural beauty, ecological significance, and cultural heritage.

In 2024, Glacier National Park remains a beacon of natural wonder, attracting visitors from around the world. With each passing year, the park's allure and importance grow, making it a must-see destination for those who love nature, history, and outdoor adventure.

Geographic and Demographic information of Glacier National Park

Glacier National Park is located in the northwest corner of Montana, USA, along the U.S.-Canada border. The park covers over 1 million acres (4,000 square kilometers) and is part of the Rocky Mountains, featuring rugged peaks, deep valleys, and over 130 named lakes. The park is home to a diverse range of ecosystems, from dense forests to alpine tundra, and is known for its stunning glaciers, though many have been shrinking due to climate change.

Geographically, the park is divided by the Continental Divide, which influences the climate and hydrology of the region. The eastern side of the park is generally drier and features more open landscapes, while the western side is wetter, with lush forests and abundant wildlife.

Demographically, Glacier National Park is a popular destination, attracting over 3 million visitors annually. The nearest towns include West Glacier, East Glacier Park Village, and St. Mary, which serve as gateways to the park. The park is managed by the National Park Service, and its remote location and rugged terrain contribute to its reputation as a wilderness area, offering opportunities for hiking, camping, and wildlife observation.

History and Significance

Glacier National Park's history is deeply intertwined with its landscapes and the indigenous peoples who have inhabited the area for thousands of years. The Blackfeet, Salish, Kootenai, and Pend d'Oreille tribes hold the land as sacred, and their cultural traditions are still evident today. European exploration began in the early 19th century, with fur traders and explorers, but it wasn't until the late 19th century, with the Great Northern Railway's expansion, that the area became accessible to settlers and tourists. Conservationists like George Bird Grinnell, known as the "Father of Glacier National Park," were instrumental in preserving the area, leading to its establishment as a national park on May 11, 1910. The park played a key role in developing tourism in the American West, with iconic lodges built by the Great Northern Railway attracting visitors worldwide. In 1932, Glacier was linked with Waterton Lakes National Park in Canada to form the world's first International Peace Park, a symbol of U.S.-Canada friendship. Today, Glacier National Park continues to be a sanctuary for diverse species and a testament to the vision of early conservationists. Its glaciers, though shrinking, still shape the landscape and remind us of the power of natural forces. For visitors, the park offers a journey through time, revealing both geological history and the cultural heritage of the indigenous peoples and early settlers.

What's New in 2024

As we move into 2024, Glacier National Park continues to evolve, offering new experiences and addressing the challenges posed by climate change, increasing visitor numbers, and the need for sustainable tourism practices. Here's what's new and noteworthy in Glacier National Park for 2024:

1. **Climate Change and Glacial Monitoring**: One of the most urgent issues facing Glacier National Park is the impact of climate change on its glaciers. In 2024, the park continues its efforts to monitor and study the glaciers that give the park its name. Visitors can expect new educational programs and exhibits focusing on glaciology and the impacts of climate change, aimed at raising awareness and encouraging conservation efforts.

2. **New and Improved Trails**: Glacier National Park is famous for its extensive network of hiking trails, and in 2024, several trails have been improved to enhance the visitor experience. The Highline Trail, one of the most popular in the park, has undergone maintenance to ensure safety and accessibility. Additionally, new interpretive signs have been added along various trails to provide hikers with information about the park's natural and cultural history.

3. **Sustainable Tourism Initiatives**: Acknowledging the need to protect its delicate ecosystems, Glacier National Park has introduced new sustainable tourism initiatives in 2024. These include expanded shuttle services to reduce the number of private vehicles on park roads, new electric vehicle charging stations, and increased recycling and waste reduction programs. The park is also encouraging visitors to participate in volunteer conservation programs, such as trail maintenance and wildlife monitoring.

4. **Enhanced Visitor Centers**: The park's visitor centers have been updated to provide more engaging and informative experiences. The Apgar Visitor Center, in particular, now features interactive exhibits that highlight the park's diverse ecosystems, wildlife, and the history of human interaction with the land. These centers also serve as hubs for ranger-led programs, offering visitors the chance to learn from experts about the park's unique features.

5. **Wildlife Conservation Programs**: Glacier National Park continues to lead in wildlife conservation, and in 2024, new initiatives are being introduced to protect vulnerable species. These include expanded monitoring programs for grizzly bears, mountain goats, and wolverines, as well as new efforts to reduce human-wildlife conflicts. Visitors can learn about these programs through guided tours and educational displays.

6. **Art and Culture Events**: In 2024, Glacier National Park is putting a greater focus on celebrating the cultural heritage of the area. The park will host a series of art and culture events throughout the year, including Native American cultural demonstrations, art exhibitions, and music performances. These events aim to enrich the visitor experience and deepen the connection to the park's history and cultural significance.

7. **Improved Accessibility**: Glacier National Park is committed to making its wonders accessible to all visitors. In 2024, the park has introduced new accessibility features, including improved wheelchair-accessible trails, additional accessible camping facilities, and enhanced services for visitors with visual or hearing impairments. The goal is to ensure that everyone, regardless of physical ability, can enjoy the beauty of Glacier National Park.

8. **Night Sky Programs**: Glacier National Park is known for its dark skies, offering some of the best stargazing opportunities in the United States. In 2024, the park is expanding its night sky programs, with more ranger-led stargazing sessions, night photography workshops, and educational programs about the importance of preserving dark skies. The park's commitment to minimizing light pollution ensures that visitors can experience the awe-inspiring beauty of the night sky.

9. **Collaborations with Local Communities**: Glacier National Park continues to strengthen its partnerships with local communities and businesses. In 2024, the park is working closely with surrounding towns to promote sustainable tourism, support local economies, and enhance visitor services. These collaborations include joint marketing efforts, community events, and initiatives to encourage visitors to explore the areas around the park.

10. **New Interpretive Programs**: To deepen visitors' understanding of Glacier National Park's natural and cultural heritage, new interpretive programs have been introduced for 2024. These programs include guided hikes, educational talks, and hands-on activities designed to engage visitors of all ages. Topics range from geology and wildlife to the history of Native American tribes in the region.

As you explore Glacier National Park in 2024, these new developments and initiatives will enhance your experience, providing more opportunities to connect with the park's landscapes, wildlife, and history. Whether you are a first-time visitor or a seasoned park enthusiast, there is always something new to discover in Glacier National Park.

How to Use This Guide

This travel guide to Glacier National Park has been thoughtfully designed to help you make the most of your visit, whether it's your first time or you're returning for another adventure. Here's how to use this guide effectively:

1. **Plan Your Visit**: Start with the "Planning Your Trip" section. Here, you'll find all the essential information on the best times to visit, how to get to the park, and what to pack. This section also covers important logistics like park fees, permits, and regulations, ensuring that you are well-prepared before you arrive.

2. **Explore the Park**: Once you're at the park, the "Navigating the Park" section will help you get your bearings. It provides detailed information on the park's entrances, major roadways, and transportation options. Whether you're driving, biking, or using the park's shuttle services, this section ensures you know how to get around efficiently and safely.

3. **Discover Top Attractions**
   "Top Attractions" chapter is your essential guide to exploring Glacier National Park's most famous sites. From the awe-inspiring Going-to-the-Sun Road to the peaceful waters of Lake McDonald, this section offers detailed descriptions, insider tips, and suggested itineraries to help you maximize your visit to these iconic locations.

4. **Hiking Adventures**: If hiking is a key part of your plans, the "Hiking in Glacier National Park" section provides comprehensive guides to the park's most popular trails. Whether you're a beginner or an experienced hiker, you'll find trail descriptions, difficulty ratings, and practical tips for each hike. The guide also includes information on backcountry permits for those interested in extended adventures.

5. **Wildlife Watching**: Glacier National Park is a haven for wildlife enthusiasts. The "Wildlife Viewing" chapter offers insights into the park's diverse animal species, the best locations for spotting them, and crucial safety tips for encounters with wildlife, particularly bears and other large mammals.

6. **Lodging and Dining**: The "Camping and Lodging" and "Dining and Shopping" sections help you find the perfect place to stay and eat. Whether you prefer camping under the stars or relaxing in a historic lodge, these chapters cover all the options. You'll also find recommendations for dining inside and near the park, along with tips for stocking up on supplies.

7. **Activities and Experiences**: For those seeking more than just sightseeing, the "Activities and Adventures" section highlights various ways to experience Glacier National Park, from guided tours and ranger programs to boating, fishing, and

winter sports. This chapter also suggests family-friendly activities and prime locations for photography.

8. **Cultural and Historical Insights**: To deepen your connection with Glacier National Park, the "Cultural and Historical Sites" section delves into the human history of the area. It explores indigenous heritage, historic lodges, and the impact of the Great Northern Railway. This section is ideal for those who want to understand the stories and people that have shaped the park.

9. **Explore Beyond the Park**: If you have extra time, the "Day Trips and Nearby Attractions" chapter offers suggestions for excursions beyond Glacier's borders. Whether you're interested in nearby towns like Whitefish and Kalispell or a cross-border visit to Canada's Waterton Lakes National Park, this chapter helps you extend your adventure beyond the park.

10. **Sustainable Travel Practices**: The "Sustainable and Responsible Travel" section emphasizes the importance of protecting Glacier National Park for future generations. It offers tips on minimizing your environmental impact, supporting local communities, and participating in volunteer opportunities.

11. **Essential Resources**: The "Travel Resources" chapter provides practical tools such as maps, must-have apps, emergency contacts, and details on visitor centers. This section ensures you have everything you need for a smooth and enjoyable visit.

12. **Reflect and Conclude**: The "Conclusion" offers final tips and reflections to help you finish your visit with a profound appreciation for Glacier National Park. It also looks ahead to the park's future, encouraging ongoing stewardship and conservation efforts.

Planning Your Trip to Glacier National Park

Planning a trip to Glacier National Park is an exciting experience, but it's important to prepare properly due to the park's remote location, changing weather, and vast wilderness. This chapter will help you plan your visit, covering the best times to go, entry fees, how to get there, what to pack, and important rules and safety tips.

Best Times to Visit

Seasonal Overview:

Glacier National Park offers something different in every season, so it's important to choose the best time for what you want to do.

- **Summer (Late June to Early September):** Summer is the most popular time to visit Glacier National Park. The weather is warm, and all the roads and trails are open. This is the best time for hiking, driving the famous Going-to-the-Sun Road, and enjoying the beautiful scenery. However, because it's so popular, the park can get crowded, so it's a good idea to book everything early.
  Key Points:
    - All facilities and roads are open.
    - Best time for hiking, wildlife viewing, and scenic drives.

- Warm weather during the day, usually between 60°F and 80°F (15°C to 27°C).
- Expect large crowds, so arrive early to avoid them.
- **Fall (Mid-September to Early November):** Fall is a quieter time to visit Glacier National Park. The weather is cooler, and the fall colors are beautiful. Many park facilities begin to close by mid-September, but with fewer visitors, it's a peaceful time to enjoy the park. Wildlife is also more active as animals prepare for winter.
  Key Points:
  - Cooler temperatures, from 30°F to 60°F (-1°C to 16°C).
  - Stunning fall colors and good wildlife viewing.
  - Some facilities and roads start to close, so check before you go.
  - Great for photography and a quieter experience.
- **Winter (Late November to March):** Winter turns Glacier National Park into a snowy wonderland. Although many roads and facilities are closed, the park remains open for winter activities like snowshoeing and cross-country skiing. Winter is the least crowded season, offering solitude, but it requires more preparation and experience in winter conditions.
  Key Points:
  - Cold, with temperatures often below freezing.
  - Limited access; most roads and facilities are closed.
  - Ideal for snowshoeing, skiing, and winter photography.
  - You need to be well-prepared for extreme cold and snow.
- **Spring (April to Early June):** Spring is a time of renewal in Glacier National Park, but it can also be unpredictable. Snow may still cover some areas, and the weather can change quickly. By late May, the lower trails open up, and the waterfalls are at their best. Spring is also a great time to see wildlife.
  Key Points:
  - Variable weather, with temperatures from 20°F to 60°F (-6°C to 16°C).
  - Melting snow means high, fast-running streams and waterfalls.
  - Limited access to higher areas; Going-to-the-Sun Road usually opens in late June.
  - Good time for wildlife viewing and early hikes.

Overall Recommendation: For most people, late June to early September is the best time to visit because everything in the park is open. However, if you prefer a quieter experience and cooler weather, mid-September to early November is also a great time.

Entry Fees and Park Passes

You need to pay an entry fee to visit Glacier National Park. The fees help maintain the park and protect its natural beauty. There are different types of passes available depending on how you plan to visit.

Entry Fees (2024 Rates):

- **Vehicle Pass:** $35 per vehicle, valid for 7 days.
  - This pass covers everyone in one vehicle and is valid for seven days.
- **Motorcycle Pass:** $30 per motorcycle, valid for 7 days.
  - This pass covers one motorcycle and any passengers for seven days.
- **Individual Pass:** $20 per person, valid for 7 days.
  - For visitors entering on foot or by bicycle, this pass is valid for seven days.
- **Annual Park Pass:** $70 per vehicle.
  - This pass allows unlimited visits to Glacier National Park for one year.
- **America the Beautiful Pass:** $80, valid for one year.
  - This pass gives access to over 2,000 federal recreation sites, including all national parks in the U.S., for one year.

Where to Buy Passes:

- **Online:** It's best to buy your pass online through the National Park Service website before your visit.
- **At the Park:** You can also buy passes at the park entrances, but there might be long lines during busy times.
- **Visitor Centers:** Passes are available at visitor centers inside the park.

Special Passes:

- **Senior Pass:** U.S. citizens or permanent residents aged 62 or older can get a Senior Pass, which offers lifetime or annual access to national parks.
- **Military Pass:** Active-duty military personnel and their dependents can get a free annual pass.
- **Access Pass:** U.S. citizens or permanent residents with permanent disabilities can get a free lifetime pass.
- **4th Grade Pass:** Fourth graders and their families can get a free annual pass through the Every Kid Outdoors program.

Key Points:

- Buy your pass online in advance to save time.

- Consider the America the Beautiful Pass if you plan to visit multiple national parks.
- Look into discounts if you're eligible for a special pass.

Getting to Glacier National Park

Glacier National Park is in a remote part of northern Montana, near the Canadian border. You can get there by car, plane, or train.

By Car:

Driving is a popular way to get to Glacier National Park because it gives you the freedom to explore at your own pace.

- **From Kalispell, MT:** The park is about 30 miles (48 km) from Kalispell, and the drive takes about 45 minutes via U.S. Route 2 East. Kalispell has the nearest airport and a variety of services.

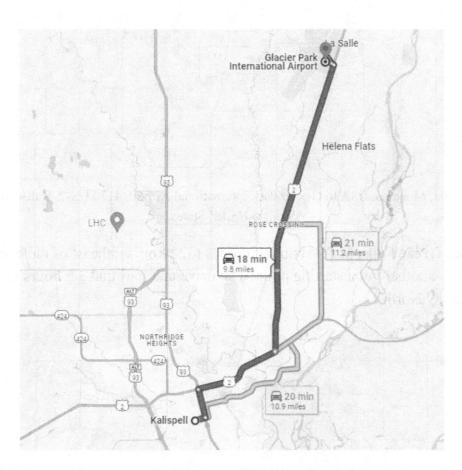

Kalispell, Montana 59901, USA to Glacier Park International Airport, 4170 US-2, Kalispell, MT 59901, United States.

- **From Missoula, MT:** The park is about 140 miles (225 km) from Missoula, which takes about 2.5 hours to drive via U.S. Route 93 North and U.S. Route 2 East. Missoula has more services and car rental options.

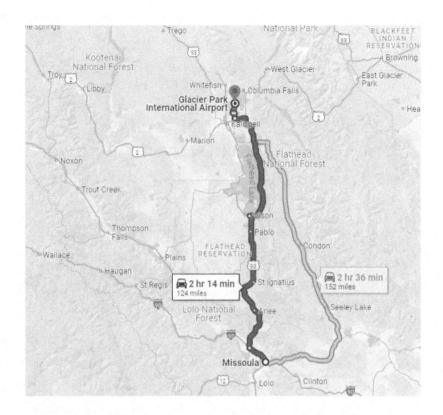

Missoula, Montana, USA to Glacier Park International Airport, 4170 US-2, Kalispell, MT 59901, United States.

- **From Great Falls, MT:** About 200 miles (322 km) southeast of the park, Great Falls is another good starting point. The drive takes around 3.5 hours via U.S. Route 89 North.

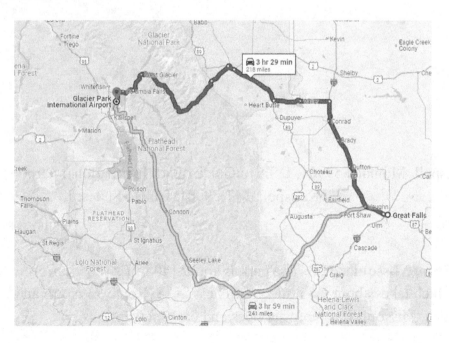

- **From Canada:** If you're coming from Canada, the park is accessible via the Chief Mountain International Highway (closed in winter). The drive from Calgary to the park's St. Mary Entrance takes about 4 hours (180 miles / 290 km).

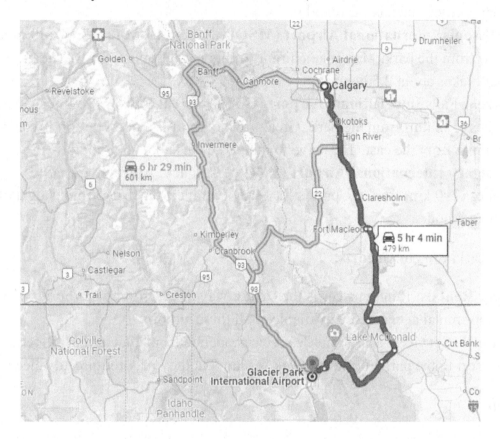

Calgary, Alberta, Canada to Glacier Park International Airport, 4170 US-2, Kalispell, MT 59901, United States

Parking and Road Conditions:

- **Parking:** Parking can be tough at popular spots during peak season, so arrive early or use the park's shuttle service.
- **Road Conditions:** Check road conditions before your trip, as snow and maintenance can cause closures or delays.

By Plane:

Flying is convenient if you're coming from far away. The nearest airports provide easy access to Glacier National Park.

- **Glacier Park International Airport (FCA) – Kalispell, MT:** About 30 miles (48 km) from the park's West Entrance, this is the closest airport. It offers flights from major cities and has car rental services.
- **Missoula International Airport (MSO) – Missoula, MT:** About 140 miles (225 km) from the park, Missoula's airport offers more flight options. The drive to the park takes about 2.5 hours.
- **Great Falls International Airport (GTF) – Great Falls, MT:** Located about 200 miles (322 km) from the park, Great Falls' airport is a good option if you're coming from the east. The drive to the park takes about 3.5 hours.
- **Calgary International Airport (YYC) – Calgary, Alberta, Canada:** About 180 miles (290 km) from the park's St. Mary Entrance, the drive from Calgary takes about 4 hours.

Transportation from Airports:

- **Car Rentals:** Renting a car is the easiest way to get from the airport to the park. Major rental agencies are available at all these airports.
- **Shuttle Services:** Some shuttle services operate from Glacier Park International Airport to the park during the peak season, but they may require advance booking.

By Train:

Traveling by train offers a scenic and unique way to reach Glacier National Park. The Amtrak Empire Builder route runs across the northern U.S. and stops near the park.

- **Amtrak's Empire Builder:** This route connects Chicago to Seattle/Portland, passing through Glacier National Park. There are several stops near the park:
  - **West Glacier Station (Belton):** Close to the West Entrance, this is the most convenient stop for visitors staying near Apgar Village or Lake McDonald.
  - **East Glacier Park Station:** Near the park's eastern entrances, this station is also close to the town of East Glacier Park, where you can find accommodations and services.
  - **Essex Station:** Located in a more remote area of the park, this station is ideal if you're planning to stay at the historic Izaak Walton Inn or explore the Middle Fork of the Flathead River.

Travel Time and Experience:

- **Travel Time:** The train journey to Glacier National Park can take several hours or even days, depending on your starting point. For example, the trip from Chicago to West Glacier takes about 30 hours, while the journey from Seattle takes around 16 hours.
- **Scenic Views:** The Empire Builder offers some of the most beautiful train views in the U.S., with stunning sights of the northern plains, Rocky Mountains, and Glacier National Park itself.

Weather and What to Pack

Glacier National Park's weather can be unpredictable, with conditions varying greatly depending on the season, elevation, and time of day. Being prepared for changing weather is key to having a safe and comfortable visit.

Seasonal Weather Overview:

- **Summer (June to September):**
  - **Weather:** Summer is generally warm, with daytime temperatures ranging from 60°F to 80°F (15°C to 27°C) at lower elevations. However, temperatures can drop significantly at higher elevations, especially at night.
  - **Rain:** Afternoon thunderstorms are common, so it's important to be ready for sudden changes in weather.
  - **Packing Essentials:** Lightweight, breathable clothing, a waterproof jacket, sturdy hiking boots, sunglasses, sunscreen, a hat, and layers for cooler evenings.
- **Fall (September to November):**
  - **Weather:** Fall brings cooler temperatures, ranging from 30°F to 60°F (-1°C to 16°C), with the possibility of early snow at higher elevations.
  - **Packing Essentials:** Warm layers, a thermal base layer, a waterproof jacket, gloves, a hat, and waterproof hiking boots.
- **Winter (November to March):**
  - **Weather:** Winter temperatures often drop below freezing, with heavy snowfall. Temperatures can range from -10°F to 30°F (-23°C to -1°C) at lower elevations, and even colder at higher elevations.

- **Packing Essentials:** Insulated clothing, a down jacket, thermal layers, waterproof snow boots, a hat, gloves, a scarf, and a high-quality sleeping bag if you're camping.
- **Spring (April to June):**
  - **Weather:** Spring is highly variable, with temperatures ranging from 20°F to 60°F (-6°C to 16°C). Snow may linger into late spring at higher elevations, and rain is frequent.
  - **Packing Essentials:** Waterproof clothing, layers for fluctuating temperatures, waterproof hiking boots, and a hat.

Special Considerations:

- **Altitude:** Glacier National Park's elevations vary from 3,150 feet (960 meters) at Lake McDonald to over 10,000 feet (3,050 meters) at the highest peaks. Higher elevations are cooler, so it's important to pack layers to stay warm.
- **Sun Protection:** The high elevation means stronger UV rays, so wear sunscreen, sunglasses, and a hat, even on cloudy days.
- **Hydration:** The dry mountain air can lead to dehydration faster than you might expect. Carry plenty of water, especially on hikes, and consider using a hydration pack for convenience.

Accessibility Information

Glacier National Park aims to be accessible to all visitors, including those with disabilities. While the park's rugged terrain can be challenging, there are various facilities and services designed to improve accessibility.

Accessible Facilities and Services:

- **Visitor Centers:** The main visitor centers, such as Apgar Visitor Center and St. Mary Visitor Center, are wheelchair accessible, with accessible restrooms, exhibits, and information desks.
- **Scenic Drives:** The Going-to-the-Sun Road is fully accessible by vehicle and offers incredible views of the park. Accessible parking spots are available at key viewpoints and visitor centers along the road.
- **Accessible Trails:**
  - **Trail of the Cedars:** Near Avalanche Creek, this fully accessible boardwalk trail takes visitors through a beautiful forest of cedar and hemlock trees, with views of Avalanche Gorge.

- ○ **Running Eagle Falls Trail:** Located in the Two Medicine area, this short, accessible trail leads to a stunning waterfall known as "Trick Falls."
  - ○ **Apgar Bike Path:** This paved, wheelchair-accessible path offers a gentle route through the forest near Apgar Village.
- **Accessible Campgrounds:** Some campgrounds, including Apgar, St. Mary, and Fish Creek, offer accessible campsites with features like accessible picnic tables, restrooms, and pathways.
- **Shuttle Service:** The park's shuttle service, which runs along the Going-to-the-Sun Road, is wheelchair accessible. This service allows visitors to explore the park without needing a personal vehicle, with shuttle stops at many popular sites.

Challenges and Considerations:

- **Terrain:** Glacier National Park's rugged terrain can be challenging for visitors with mobility issues. Many trails are steep, rocky, or uneven, so some areas may not be accessible without assistance.
- **Limited Accessibility in Remote Areas:** More remote parts of the park, such as backcountry campsites or high-elevation trails, may not be accessible to all visitors. It's a good idea to plan ahead and talk to park staff for advice on accessible options.

Permits and Reservations

Getting the right permits and reservations is essential for a smooth trip to Glacier National Park, especially if you plan to camp, hike in the backcountry, or drive the Going-to-the-Sun Road during busy times. Knowing the process ahead of time will help you avoid any issues.

Backcountry Camping Permits:

If you plan to camp overnight in the backcountry, you'll need a backcountry camping permit.

- **Permit Requirements:** A permit is required for all overnight stays in Glacier's backcountry. Permits are issued on a first-come, first-served basis at park visitor centers or ranger stations.
- **Reservation System:** Up to 70% of backcountry camping permits can be reserved in advance through Recreation.gov. The remaining permits are available as walk-ins on the day before or the day of your hike.

- **Cost:** In 2024, backcountry camping permits cost $10 per night, plus a $7 per person, per night fee. Reservation fees apply for advance bookings.
- **Best Practices:** Backcountry camping is very popular, so it's best to reserve permits as early as possible, especially for popular routes like the North Circle or Continental Divide Trail. If you don't have a reservation, arrive early at a ranger station to get a walk-in permit.

Going-to-the-Sun Road Vehicle Reservations:

To manage high demand and protect the visitor experience, Glacier National Park requires vehicle reservations to drive the Going-to-the-Sun Road during peak season.

- **Reservation Period:** Vehicle reservations are required from late June to early September. The exact dates change each year depending on road conditions and snowmelt.
- **Reservation Process:** Reservations can be made through Recreation.gov starting in March. A limited number of reservations are also released 24 hours in advance. This is in addition to the park entry fee.
- **Cost:** The cost for a vehicle reservation is $2, on top of the park entry fee.
- **Key Considerations:** Reservations sell out quickly, so plan ahead. If you can't get a reservation, consider using the park's shuttle service, which doesn't require a reservation.

Camping Reservations:

Glacier National Park has several campgrounds, and many require reservations during the busy season.

- **Reservable Campgrounds:** Apgar, Fish Creek, Many Glacier, and St. Mary campgrounds allow reservations. You can book them up to six months in advance on Recreation.gov.
- **First-Come, First-Served Campgrounds:** Some campgrounds, like Avalanche, Rising Sun, and Two Medicine, operate on a first-come, first-served basis. It's best to arrive early in the day to secure a spot, especially during summer.
- **Cost:** Campground fees range from $10 to $23 per night, depending on the location. Group sites and reservations might have extra fees.
- **Key Tips:** For popular campgrounds like Many Glacier, book as early as possible. For a more spontaneous trip, check campground status online or at visitor centers for available spots.

Special Use Permits:

If you're planning activities beyond general recreation, like weddings, commercial filming, or special events, you'll need a special use permit.

- **Application Process:** Special use permits should be applied for well in advance. You can submit applications through the park's administrative offices.
- **Cost:** Fees vary depending on the activity. You may need insurance or bonds for certain events.
- **Considerations:** Special use permits are subject to approval based on park guidelines and the potential impact on resources and other visitors.

Safety Tips and Guidelines

Staying safe in Glacier National Park is crucial to enjoying your visit. The park's rugged terrain, unpredictable weather, and abundant wildlife require you to be prepared and cautious at all times.

Wildlife Safety:

Glacier National Park is home to many wild animals, including grizzly bears, black bears, mountain lions, moose, and bighorn sheep. While seeing wildlife is exciting, it's important to follow safety guidelines to avoid dangerous situations.

- **Bear Safety:** Bears are common in Glacier National Park, and you need to be prepared for encounters:
    - **Carry Bear Spray:** Bear spray is an effective tool for deterring bears. Keep it accessible and know how to use it.
    - **Make Noise:** When hiking, especially in dense areas or near streams, make noise to avoid surprising bears. Clap, talk loudly, or use a bell.
    - **Travel in Groups:** Bears are less likely to approach groups. If possible, hike with at least three or four people.
    - **Store Food Properly:** Never leave food, garbage, or scented items unattended. Use bear-proof containers or hang food in a tree at least 10 feet off the ground and 4 feet away from the trunk.
- **Mountain Lion Safety:** Mountain lions are more elusive but can be dangerous:
    - **Keep Children Close:** Children should always stay within your sight and close to you.

- ○ **Don't Run:** If you encounter a mountain lion, do not run. Instead, make yourself look larger and speak firmly.
  - ○ **Fight Back:** If a mountain lion attacks, fight back using any available objects.
- **Moose Safety:** Moose are large and unpredictable. Keep a safe distance, especially if the moose shows signs of aggression (ears back, hair raised, or bluff charges).

Hiking Safety:

- **Trail Conditions:** Always check trail conditions before setting out. Some trails may be closed due to weather, wildlife activity, or maintenance.
- **Stay on Trails:** To protect the environment and for your safety, always stay on designated trails.
- **Carry a Map and Compass:** Cell service is limited in the park, so don't rely on your phone for navigation. Carry a detailed map and compass, and know how to use them.
- **Weather Awareness:** Weather can change quickly in the mountains. Be prepared for sudden rain, wind, or cold, and always carry appropriate gear.
- **Hydration and Nutrition:** Bring plenty of water and snacks, especially on long hikes. Dehydration and fatigue can set in quickly, particularly at higher elevations.

Water Safety:

Glacier National Park is known for its beautiful lakes, rivers, and waterfalls, but these water features can be dangerous.

- **Cold Water:** Even in summer, the water is extremely cold, and hypothermia can occur quickly. Avoid swimming unless you are well-prepared.
- **Swift Currents:** Rivers and streams can have fast currents, especially during spring snowmelt. Be cautious when crossing or wading through water.
- **Waterborne Illnesses:** Always filter or treat water from natural sources before drinking to prevent waterborne illnesses like Giardia.

General Safety Tips:

- **Emergency Contacts:** Program the park's emergency contact numbers into your phone. For emergencies, dial 911. For non-life-threatening issues, contact park rangers at visitor centers.

- **Insect Protection:** Carry insect repellent to protect against mosquitoes and ticks, especially in the summer.
- **Leave No Trace:** Follow Leave No Trace principles by packing out all trash, minimizing campfire impact, and respecting wildlife and other visitors.

Park Regulations

To protect Glacier National Park's natural beauty and ensure everyone has a safe and enjoyable visit, the park has specific rules and regulations. Knowing and following these rules will help preserve the park for future visitors and prevent any legal issues during your trip.

General Park Rules:

- **Wildlife Protection:** It is illegal to feed, harass, or approach wildlife. Keep a distance of at least 100 yards (91 meters) from bears and wolves, and 25 yards (23 meters) from other wildlife.
- **Leave No Trace:** Visitors must pack out all trash and leave no trace of their visit. This includes properly disposing of waste and respecting campsite regulations.
- **Fire Regulations:** Campfires are only allowed in designated fire grates in established campgrounds. Never leave a fire unattended, and ensure it is fully extinguished before leaving.

Camping Regulations:

- **Backcountry Camping:** A permit is required for all backcountry camping, and campers must use designated campsites. Follow all food storage guidelines to avoid attracting wildlife.
- **Quiet Hours:** Most campgrounds enforce quiet hours from 10 PM to 6 AM to ensure a peaceful environment for all visitors.
- **Length of Stay:** The maximum stay at any campground is usually 14 days, but some campgrounds may have shorter limits during peak season.

Hiking and Trail Use:

- **Stay on Trails:** Always stay on designated trails to protect the environment and for your safety.

- **Group Size:** Group size for hiking and camping may be limited, especially in backcountry areas, to minimize environmental impact and maintain a wilderness experience for all visitors.

Pet Regulations:

- **Pets on Leash:** Pets must be kept on a leash no longer than six feet (1.8 meters) at all times. Pets are not allowed on trails, in the backcountry, or in buildings, but are permitted in campgrounds, picnic areas, and along roads.
- **Pet Waste:** Pet owners are responsible for cleaning up after their pets. Waste should be disposed of in trash receptacles.

Bicycling Rules:

- **Trail Restrictions:** Bicycles are only allowed on paved roads and designated bike paths, not on trails. The park's roads can be narrow and winding, so cyclists should use caution and wear helmets.
- **Time Restrictions on Going-to-the-Sun Road:** Bicycles are restricted on certain sections of Going-to-the-Sun Road during peak hours (typically between 11 AM and 4 PM) due to heavy traffic. Check the park's website or visitor centers for current restrictions.

Fishing Regulations:

- **Fishing Permits:** No fishing license is required to fish in Glacier National Park, but specific regulations regarding catch limits, methods, and seasons apply. Some waters are catch-and-release only.
- **Aquatic Invasive Species:** To protect the park's waterways, all watercraft (including boats, kayaks, and paddleboards) must be inspected for aquatic invasive species before being launched in park waters.

Drone Use:

- **Prohibited:** The use of drones or unmanned aircraft within Glacier National Park is prohibited to protect wildlife and the natural soundscape.

Cultural and Historical Sites:

- **Respect Historical Artifacts:** Do not disturb or remove any cultural or historical artifacts. All artifacts, no matter how small, are protected by law.

- **Photography and Filming:** While personal photography is encouraged, commercial filming and photography require a special use permit.

Special Use Permits:

- **Events and Gatherings:** Any organized event or gathering, such as weddings or group activities, may require a special use permit. These permits must be obtained in advance, and there are restrictions on the size and location of such events to minimize impact on the park.

Respect for Indigenous Lands:

- **Cultural Sensitivity:** Glacier National Park is on the traditional lands of the Blackfeet, Salish, and Kootenai tribes. Visitors should respect the cultural significance of the land and honor all cultural sites and practices.

Navigating the Park: Glacier National Park

Navigating Glacier National Park is an essential part of your journey. With its vast expanse of over a million acres, numerous entrances, and a variety of transportation options, understanding how to get around the park will enhance your experience. This chapter delves into the layout of Glacier National Park, the key entrances and gateways, and the various ways to explore its stunning landscapes, ensuring you make the most of your visit.

Overview of Glacier National Park

Glacier National Park, located in the northwest corner of Montana near the Canadian border, is part of the Rocky Mountains and known for its stunning natural beauty. Covering over 1,500 square miles, the park features rugged mountains, pristine lakes, dense forests, and remnants of glaciers. It is divided into distinct regions, including West Glacier, St. Mary, Many Glacier, Two Medicine, and the North Fork, with the Going-to-the-Sun Road serving as its main thoroughfare. The park is also part of the Waterton-Glacier International Peace Park, a UNESCO World Heritage Site that spans the U.S.-Canada border and symbolizes peace and cooperation between the two nations.

Getting Around: Roads and Transportation

Once inside Glacier National Park, there are several ways to get around, each offering different perspectives and experiences. Whether you're driving, taking the shuttle, or biking, understanding the park's transportation options will help you plan your visit more effectively.

1. Going-to-the-Sun Road

- **Location:** West Glacier to St. Mary, Glacier National Park

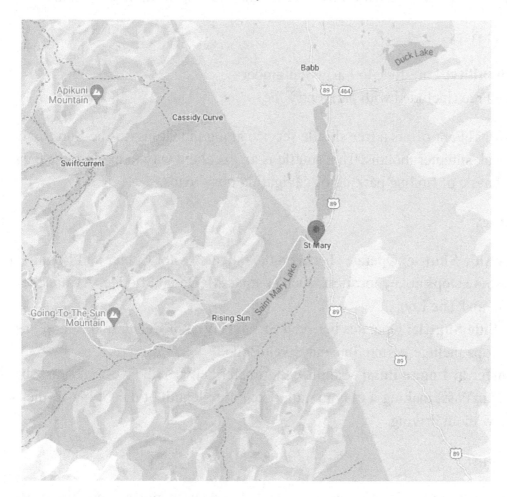

- **Length:** 50 miles (80 kilometers)
- **Elevation:** Reaches up to 6,646 feet (2,025 meters) at Logan Pass

The Going-to-the-Sun Road is the most famous and scenic road in Glacier National Park, and it's one of the highlights of any visit. This 50-mile (80-kilometer) road spans the width of the park, from the West Glacier Entrance to the St. Mary Entrance, crossing the Continental Divide at Logan Pass.

Parking: Parking along the Going-to-the-Sun Road can be challenging, especially at popular spots like Logan Pass. Arriving early in the day or later in the afternoon increases your chances of finding a parking spot.

Vehicle Restrictions: Due to the narrow and winding nature of the road, there are vehicle size restrictions on the Going-to-the-Sun Road. Vehicles, including trailers and RVs, must be no longer than 21 feet (6.4 meters) and no wider than 8 feet (2.4 meters), including mirrors. Check the park's website for the most up-to-date restrictions.

2. Shuttle Services

- **Availability:** Late June to Early September
- **Cost:** Free (included with park entry fee)

Glacier National Park offers a free shuttle service along the Going-to-the-Sun Road during the peak summer months. This shuttle is an excellent way to explore the park without the hassle of finding parking or navigating busy roads.

Shuttle Routes:

- **West Side Shuttle:** Operates between the Apgar Visitor Center and Logan Pass. This route stops at key locations such as Lake McDonald Lodge, Avalanche Creek, and The Loop.
- **East Side Shuttle:** Operates between St. Mary Visitor Center and Logan Pass. Key stops include Rising Sun and Siyeh Bend.
- **Transfer at Logan Pass:** Visitors can transfer between the west and east shuttles at Logan Pass, making it easy to travel the entire length of the Going-to-the-Sun Road without driving.

Considerations:

- **Shuttle Capacity:** Shuttles can be crowded, especially during peak times. Be prepared for possible wait times at popular stops.
- **Limited Stops:** While the shuttle covers major points along the Going-to-the-Sun Road, it doesn't stop at every trailhead or overlook. Plan your day accordingly.

3. Biking in the Park

- **Biking Season:** Late June to Early September (depending on snow conditions)
- **Biking on Roads:** Permitted on paved roads, including the Going-to-the-Sun Road

Biking is a popular way to experience Glacier National Park, offering a more intimate connection with the park's landscapes. However, due to the challenging terrain and narrow roads, it's important to plan your ride carefully.

Key Routes:

- **Going-to-the-Sun Road:** Biking this iconic road is a challenging but rewarding experience. Cyclists should be prepared for steep climbs, particularly on the west side of the road. The views along the way, especially near Logan Pass, are unmatched.
- **Apgar Bike Path:** This paved path near Apgar Village is perfect for a more relaxed ride. It's relatively flat and offers beautiful views of Lake McDonald and the surrounding forest.
- **North Fork Road:** For those seeking a less-traveled route, North Fork Road offers a quieter biking experience. This gravel road leads to the remote North Fork area of the park, where you can explore Bowman Lake and Polebridge.

Time Restrictions:

- **Going-to-the-Sun Road:** Bicycles are restricted on certain sections of the Going-to-the-Sun Road between 11 AM and 4 PM due to heavy traffic. These restrictions apply between Apgar Campground and Sprague Creek Campground, and between Logan Creek and Logan Pass.

Safety Considerations:

- **Traffic:** The narrow and winding roads in Glacier National Park can be challenging for cyclists. Always ride defensively, wear a helmet, and use lights or reflectors to increase visibility.
- **Weather:** Weather conditions can change rapidly, especially at higher elevations. Be prepared for sudden rain, wind, or cold temperatures.
- **Fitness Level:** Biking in Glacier is physically demanding, especially on steep inclines. Make sure you're in good shape and accustomed to mountain biking before attempting longer rides.

Exploration of Major Entrances and Gateways

Understanding the main entrances and gateways to Glacier National Park is essential for planning your trip, as each offers unique access points to different park regions. Here, we dive deeper into the specifics of the major entrances: West Glacier, St. Mary, Many Glacier, and Two Medicine. Each of these areas provides a different perspective of the park, catering to various interests and activities.

West Glacier Entrance

- **Location:** West Glacier, MT
- **Nearby Town:** West Glacier, a small town with basic amenities, including lodging, restaurants, and gear shops.
- **Main Attractions:** Lake McDonald, Apgar Village, Trail of the Cedars, Avalanche Lake

Highlights:

- **Lake McDonald:** This is the largest lake in Glacier National Park, renowned for its clear waters and picturesque surroundings. The lake is a hub for various activities such as kayaking, paddleboarding, and boat tours. The colorful rocks visible through the water are a favorite for photographers.

- **Apgar Village:** Just inside the West Glacier Entrance, Apgar Village offers amenities such as a visitor center, gift shops, and lodging. It's a great starting point for your journey into the park.
- **Trail of the Cedars:** Located near Avalanche Creek, this easy, accessible trail is a must-see. The boardwalk trail winds through a dense forest of ancient western red cedars and offers views of Avalanche Gorge.
- **Avalanche Lake:** A moderately challenging hike from the Trail of the Cedars leads to Avalanche Lake, a stunning alpine lake surrounded by towering cliffs and waterfalls.

Best Time to Visit:

- Summer (June to September) is the best time to visit, as all facilities are open, and the Going-to-the-Sun Road is fully accessible from this entrance.

St. Mary Entrance

- **Location:** St. Mary, MT
- **Nearby Town:** St. Mary, offering a range of services including hotels, campgrounds, and dining options.
- **Main Attractions:** St. Mary Lake, Logan Pass, Sun Point, Going-to-the-Sun Road (East Side)

Highlights:

- **St. Mary Lake:** The second-largest lake in Glacier National Park, St. Mary Lake is known for its brilliant turquoise waters and panoramic views. Boat tours are available and offer a unique way to see the surrounding peaks.
- **Logan Pass:** A 30-mile drive from the St. Mary Entrance, Logan Pass is the highest point on the Going-to-the-Sun Road. It's a prime location for spotting wildlife and offers access to the Hidden Lake Overlook and Highline Trail.
- **Sun Point:** Located along the Going-to-the-Sun Road, Sun Point provides spectacular views of St. Mary Lake and the surrounding mountains. It's also a great spot for picnicking or starting a hike along the lakeshore.

Best Time to Visit:

- Late June through September is ideal when the Going-to-the-Sun Road is open, providing full access to Logan Pass and other highlights.

Key Points:

- **Spectacular Sunrises:** St. Mary Lake is especially beautiful at sunrise, with the sun illuminating the surrounding peaks.
- **Gateway to Logan Pass:** The St. Mary Entrance is the most direct route to Logan Pass, making it a popular choice for those eager to hike or view wildlife at higher elevations.
- **Accommodation Options:** The town of St. Mary offers more lodging options than some other park entrances, making it a good base for exploring the park.

Many Glacier Entrance

- **Location:** Babb, MT
- **Nearby Town:** Babb, a small town with basic amenities. The Many Glacier area has more extensive services, including lodging and dining at the Many Glacier Hotel.
- **Main Attractions:** Many Glacier Hotel, Swiftcurrent Lake, Grinnell Glacier, Iceberg Lake

Highlights:

- **Many Glacier Hotel:** This historic hotel is one of the park's most iconic lodges, offering stunning views of Swiftcurrent Lake and the surrounding mountains. It's a great place to stay or simply visit for a meal or a boat tour.
- **Swiftcurrent Lake:** Located right next to the Many Glacier Hotel, Swiftcurrent Lake is a beautiful spot for boating, fishing, or simply relaxing by the water. Several hiking trails start from this area, making it a perfect base for exploration.
- **Grinnell Glacier:** One of the most popular hikes in the park, the trail to Grinnell Glacier offers breathtaking views of alpine meadows, lakes, and the glacier itself. It's a moderately challenging hike but well worth the effort.
- **Iceberg Lake:** Another popular hike, the trail to Iceberg Lake takes you through stunning mountain scenery to a lake often filled with floating icebergs, even in summer.

Best Time to Visit:

- July and August are the best times to visit Many Glacier, as the trails are snow-free and the weather is ideal for hiking and exploring the area's many natural attractions. However, it's also the busiest time, so early planning and reservations are essential.

Two Medicine Entrance

- **Location:** East Glacier Park, MT
- **Nearby Town:** East Glacier Park, a small town offering lodging, dining, and basic amenities.
- **Main Attractions:** Two Medicine Lake, Running Eagle Falls, Dawson-Pitamakan Loop, Scenic Boat Tours

Highlights:

- **Two Medicine Lake:** Surrounded by rugged peaks, Two Medicine Lake is a serene and less crowded alternative to the more popular areas of the park. The lake is perfect for canoeing, kayaking, and picnicking. Scenic boat tours are available and offer an excellent way to take in the surrounding landscape.
- **Running Eagle Falls:** Also known as Trick Falls, this unique waterfall appears to emerge from the middle of a cliff. It's an easy hike from the trailhead and a great spot for photography.
- **Dawson-Pitamakan Loop:** For experienced hikers, this challenging loop offers some of the most spectacular views in the park. The trail traverses high mountain passes and provides panoramic views of the surrounding valleys and peaks.
- **Cultural Significance:** The Two Medicine area is rich in Native American history and cultural significance. Visitors are encouraged to learn about the Blackfeet Nation, whose ancestral lands include this region.

Best Time to Visit:

- June through September is the best time to visit Two Medicine. The area is less crowded than other parts of the park, making it ideal for those seeking solitude and a more peaceful experience.

Top Attractions in Glacier National Park

Glacier National Park, known as the "Crown of the Continent," is a treasure trove of stunning natural beauty and outdoor adventures. The park is home to some of the most breathtaking landscapes in the United States, featuring towering mountains, pristine lakes, dense forests, and iconic glaciers. This chapter provides an in-depth exploration of the top attractions within Glacier National Park, offering insights into what makes each location unique, how to access these sites, and tips for making the most of your visit.

Going-to-the-Sun Road

- **Location:** West Glacier to St. Mary, Glacier National Park
- **Length:** 50 miles (80 kilometers)
- **Elevation:** 6,646 feet (2,025 meters) at Logan Pass
- **Entry Fee:** $35 per vehicle, valid for 7 days
- **Season:** Typically open from late June to mid-September, depending on weather conditions.

The Going-to-the-Sun Road is the crown jewel of Glacier National Park and a must-see for every visitor. This 50-mile road is an engineering marvel, cutting across the park from west to east, and offering some of the most stunning views in the United States. The road takes you through a wide range of ecosystems, from lush forests and glacial lakes to alpine tundra, with several iconic stops along the way.

Highlights:

- **Scenic Drive:** The road itself is a destination, offering jaw-dropping views of the park's most iconic landscapes. As you drive, you'll see everything from towering peaks to deep valleys and sparkling lakes.
- **Key Viewpoints:** Don't miss stops like The Loop, with its hairpin turn offering sweeping views, the Weeping Wall, where water cascades over a cliff onto the road, and the Garden Wall, a sheer cliff face covered in wildflowers in the summer.
- **Historic Significance:** The road was completed in 1932 and has been designated a National Historic Landmark, representing one of the first attempts to design a road that blends with the natural landscape.

Tips for Visiting:

- **Best Time to Visit:** To avoid the heaviest traffic, try to drive the road early in the morning or later in the afternoon. The lighting is also better for photography during these times.
- **Parking:** Parking can be a challenge at popular spots like Logan Pass, so it's best to start your day early or visit during less busy times.
- **Vehicle Restrictions:** Because the road is narrow and winding, vehicles over 21 feet long and 8 feet wide are not allowed. Consider using the park's shuttle service if your vehicle exceeds these limits.

Logan Pass

- **Location:** Along the Going-to-the-Sun Road, Glacier National Park

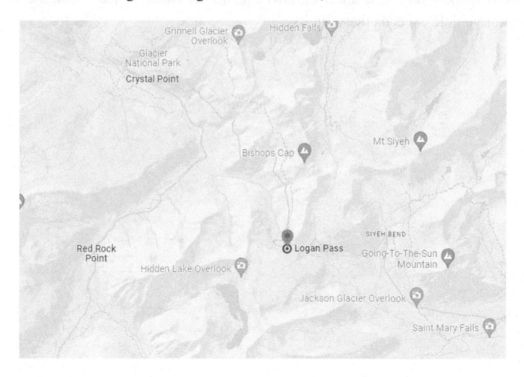

- **Elevation:** 6,646 feet (2,025 meters)
- **Parking:** Free, but spaces are limited, especially during peak hours.
- **Season:** Typically accessible from late June to mid-September.

Logan Pass is the highest point on the Going-to-the-Sun Road and one of Glacier National Park's most iconic destinations. Nestled in the heart of the park, the pass offers visitors a chance to experience the rugged beauty of Glacier's high country, with breathtaking views, abundant wildlife, and access to some of the park's most famous hiking trails.

Highlights:

- **Stunning Views:** From Logan Pass, you can see for miles in every direction. The surrounding peaks, including Clements Mountain and Reynolds Mountain, frame the scene, while the alpine meadows are often carpeted with wildflowers in the summer.
- **Hidden Lake Overlook:** One of the most popular hikes from Logan Pass, the trail to Hidden Lake Overlook offers spectacular views of the lake and the surrounding mountains. It's a relatively short hike, making it accessible to most visitors.
- **Highline Trail:** Another trail that starts at Logan Pass, the Highline Trail is a must for serious hikers. This trail follows the Garden Wall and offers some of the best views in the park, including close-up looks at glaciers and wildflower-covered slopes.
- **Wildlife Viewing:** Logan Pass is a great place to see wildlife, including mountain goats, bighorn sheep, and, occasionally, grizzly bears. The animals here are often accustomed to visitors, offering excellent opportunities for photography.

Tips for Visiting:

- **Arrive Early:** Parking at Logan Pass fills up quickly, especially during the summer. Plan to arrive early in the morning or later in the afternoon to secure a spot.
- **Dress in Layers:** The weather at Logan Pass can change rapidly, with temperatures often cooler than lower elevations. Be prepared for chilly winds, even in summer.
- **Safety:** Stay on designated trails to protect the fragile alpine environment and avoid disturbing wildlife.

Lake McDonald

- **Location:** West Glacier, Glacier National Park

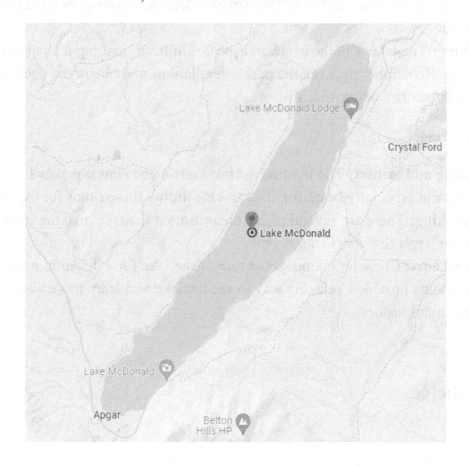

- **Length:** 10 miles (16 kilometers)
- **Max Depth:** 472 feet (144 meters)
- **Entry Fee:** $35 per vehicle, valid for 7 days

Lake McDonald is the largest lake in Glacier National Park and one of its most beautiful spots. Located near the West Glacier Entrance, the lake is surrounded by forested mountains and offers visitors a peaceful setting for a variety of outdoor activities.

Highlights:

- **Clear Waters:** The crystal-clear waters of Lake McDonald reflect the surrounding mountains, making it a favorite spot for photographers. The lake's colorful rocks, visible through the water, add to its unique charm.
- **Boating and Kayaking:** Lake McDonald is a popular spot for boating and kayaking. Canoes, kayaks, and motorboats are available for rent at Apgar Village, and the calm waters make it an ideal place to explore by boat.
- **Lake McDonald Lodge:** This historic lodge, built in 1913, is located on the eastern shore of the lake. The lodge is a great place to stay or stop for a meal, with its rustic architecture and cozy atmosphere offering a taste of early 20th-century park life.
- **Fishing:** The lake is home to several species of trout, making it a popular spot for fishing. Remember to check the park's regulations and obtain the necessary permits before casting your line.

Tips for Visiting:

- **Sunrise and Sunset:** The lighting during sunrise and sunset makes Lake McDonald especially beautiful. Plan to visit during these times for the best photos.
- **Picnicking:** There are several picnic areas around the lake, making it a perfect spot for a relaxing meal with a view.
- **Boat Tours:** Consider taking a boat tour of the lake for a different perspective. These tours provide a relaxing way to see the lake and learn more about its natural and cultural history.

Two Medicine

- **Location:** Southeastern Glacier National Park, near East Glacier Park, MT

- **Entry Fee:** $35 per vehicle, valid for 7 days

Two Medicine is one of Glacier National Park's hidden gems, offering visitors a quieter, more secluded experience compared to the busier areas like Many Glacier and Going-to-the-Sun Road. The Two Medicine area is rich in natural beauty, with stunning lakes, towering peaks, and excellent hiking opportunities.

Highlights:

- **Two Medicine Lake:** The centerpiece of the area, Two Medicine Lake is surrounded by jagged peaks and offers a peaceful setting for boating, fishing, and picnicking. Boat tours are available and provide a unique perspective of the lake and surrounding mountains.
- **Running Eagle Falls:** Also known as Trick Falls, this waterfall appears to flow out of the middle of a cliff during the spring and early summer when the water level is high. It's an easy, family-friendly hike from the trailhead to the falls.
- **Scenic Trails:** The Two Medicine area is home to several excellent hiking trails, including the Aster Park Overlook, Twin Falls, and the challenging Dawson-Pitamakan Loop, which offers some of the best views in the park.
- **Cultural Significance:** Two Medicine is an area of historical and cultural importance to the Blackfeet Nation. Visitors are encouraged to learn about the history and cultural significance of this area.

Tips for Visiting:

- **Avoid the Crowds:** Two Medicine is less crowded than other parts of the park, making it a great choice if you're looking for a quieter experience. Visit during the week if possible to avoid even smaller crowds.
- **Prepare for Hiking:** Whether you're tackling a short walk or a challenging backcountry trek, make sure you're prepared with the right gear and plenty of water and snacks.
- **Explore by Boat:** Consider renting a canoe or taking a boat tour to fully appreciate the beauty of Two Medicine Lake.

Avalanche Lake

- **Location:** West Glacier, along the Going-to-the-Sun Road

- **Trail Length:** 4.5 miles (7.2 kilometers) round trip
- **Elevation Gain:** 730 feet (222 meters)
- **Difficulty:** Moderate

Avalanche Lake is one of the most popular hiking destinations in Glacier National Park, and for good reason. The trail to Avalanche Lake is relatively short and easy, making it accessible to most visitors, while the lake itself is a stunning reward at the end of the hike.

Highlights:

- **Trail of the Cedars:** The hike to Avalanche Lake begins along the Trail of the Cedars, a boardwalk path that winds through an old-growth forest of towering cedar and hemlock trees. The cool, shaded trail is particularly enjoyable on a hot summer day.
- **Avalanche Gorge:** As you hike along the trail, you'll pass Avalanche Gorge, where the Avalanche Creek cuts through a narrow canyon. The swirling water and carved rock walls make this a popular spot for photos.
- **Avalanche Lake:** At the end of the trail, you'll arrive at Avalanche Lake, a stunning alpine lake surrounded by steep cliffs and waterfalls. The tranquil waters of the lake reflect the surrounding mountains, creating a scene straight out of a postcard.
- **Wildlife:** While the trail is popular and often busy, it's not uncommon to see wildlife along the way, including deer, mountain goats, and the occasional bear.

Tips for Visiting:

- **Start Early:** The trail to Avalanche Lake is one of the most popular in the park, and the parking area fills up quickly. Start your hike early in the morning to avoid the crowds and the heat.
- **Pack a Picnic:** Avalanche Lake is a great spot for a picnic. Bring some snacks or a packed lunch and enjoy the scenery before heading back.
- **Prepare for the Hike:** While the trail is moderate, it does have some elevation gain. Wear sturdy shoes and bring plenty of water.

Apgar Village

- **Location:** West Glacier, Glacier National Park

- **Entry Fee:** $35 per vehicle, valid for 7 days
- **Accommodations:** Apgar Village Lodge, campgrounds

Apgar Village is located near the West Glacier Entrance and is one of the most popular hubs in Glacier National Park. It serves as the gateway to the park's western side, offering a range of services, accommodations, and easy access to Lake McDonald and other attractions.

Highlights:

- **Visitor Center:** The Apgar Visitor Center is a great place to start your visit. Here, you can get maps, check on trail conditions, and learn more about the park through interactive exhibits. Rangers are available to answer questions and provide recommendations.
- **Lake McDonald:** Just a short walk from Apgar Village, Lake McDonald is the largest lake in the park. The village's location on the lake's shore makes it an ideal spot for water activities like kayaking, paddleboarding, and boat tours.
- **Shopping and Dining:** Apgar Village offers several shops where you can purchase souvenirs, snacks, and supplies. There are also a few dining options, including cafes and restaurants with views of the lake.
- **Apgar Campground:** One of the largest campgrounds in the park, Apgar Campground offers a convenient place to stay, with easy access to all the amenities in the village and nearby trails.

Tips for Visiting:

- **Book Early:** Accommodations in Apgar Village, including the campground, fill up quickly, especially during the summer months. Reserve your spot as early as possible.
- **Explore by Bike:** Rent a bike in the village and explore the Apgar Bike Path, which offers an easy ride with scenic views of the surrounding forest and Lake McDonald.
- **Family-Friendly:** Apgar Village is a great place for families, with plenty of activities and easy access to the park's attractions.

Hiking in Glacier National Park

Hiking is one of the best ways to explore Glacier National Park's natural beauty. With over 700 miles of trails, ranging from easy walks to tough backcountry routes, there's something for everyone. This guide will help you discover some of the best hikes in the park, organized by difficulty, and provide important tips to ensure a safe and enjoyable experience.

Introduction to Hiking in Glacier National Park

Glacier National Park is a hiker's dream, with trails that take you through dense forests, up mountain passes, and to stunning viewpoints. The park's varied terrain includes lush valleys, clear lakes, towering mountains, and remnants of ancient glaciers. Whether you want a short, easy walk or a multi-day backpacking trip, Glacier has a trail for you.

Best Hikes for Beginners

If you're new to hiking or just want an easy introduction to Glacier's trails, these beginner-friendly hikes offer great views without too much effort.

1. Trail of the Cedars

- **Location:** Near the West Glacier Entrance
- **Trail Length:** 0.8 miles (1.3 kilometers) round trip
- **Elevation Gain:** Minimal
- **Difficulty:** Easy
- **Parking:** Free, near the trailhead
- **Highlights:** Ancient cedar trees, Avalanche Creek

The Trail of the Cedars is perfect for beginners, offering a short, easy loop through a forest of old cedar and hemlock trees. The trail is wheelchair accessible and suitable for all ages. The boardwalk path runs alongside Avalanche Creek, where you can see clear water flowing through a narrow gorge. The cool, shaded trail is especially nice on hot days.

2. Avalanche Lake

- **Location:** Starts at the Trail of the Cedars, West Glacier
- **Trail Length:** 4.5 miles (7.2 kilometers) round trip
- **Elevation Gain:** 730 feet (222 meters)

- **Difficulty:** Moderate
- **Parking:** Free, at the Trail of the Cedars parking area
- **Highlights:** Avalanche Gorge, alpine lake, mountain views

This trail begins at the Trail of the Cedars and continues through a forest to a stunning alpine lake. The hike is fairly easy and ends at Avalanche Lake, which is surrounded by steep cliffs and waterfalls. It's a popular trail, so try to start early to avoid crowds.

3. Hidden Lake Overlook

- **Location:** Logan Pass, along the Going-to-the-Sun Road
- **Trail Length:** 2.7 miles (4.3 kilometers) round trip
- **Elevation Gain:** 540 feet (165 meters)
- **Difficulty:** Easy to Moderate
- **Parking:** Free, at Logan Pass Visitor Center
- **Highlights:** Alpine meadows, panoramic views, wildlife

The Hidden Lake Overlook is a short, rewarding hike that starts at Logan Pass. The trail goes through beautiful alpine meadows filled with wildflowers, and the view of Hidden Lake at the end is breathtaking. You're likely to see mountain goats, marmots, and maybe even a bear.

Moderate Hikes

If you're looking for something a bit more challenging, these moderate hikes offer beautiful scenery with a manageable distance and elevation gain.

1. Highline Trail

- **Location:** Starts at Logan Pass, along the Going-to-the-Sun Road
- **Trail Length:** 7.6 miles (12.2 kilometers) one way to Granite Park Chalet
- **Elevation Gain:** 800 feet (244 meters)
- **Difficulty:** Moderate
- **Parking:** Free, at Logan Pass Visitor Center
- **Highlights:** Scenic views, wildflowers, wildlife

The Highline Trail is one of the most popular hikes in Glacier, offering incredible views along the Garden Wall. The trail begins at Logan Pass and follows the Continental Divide, with stunning views of the park's rugged terrain. You'll pass fields of wildflowers and might see mountain goats and bighorn sheep. The trail ends at Granite Park Chalet, a great spot to rest before heading back.

2. Grinnell Glacier Trail

- **Location:** Many Glacier Area
- **Trail Length:** 7.6 miles (12.2 kilometers) round trip
- **Elevation Gain:** 1,600 feet (488 meters)
- **Difficulty:** Moderate to Strenuous
- **Parking:** Free, at Many Glacier Hotel
- **Highlights:** Alpine lakes, glacier views, wildlife

The Grinnell Glacier Trail is one of Glacier's most iconic hikes, with stunning views of Grinnell Glacier, Lake Josephine, and Swiftcurrent Lake. The trail is moderately challenging with some steep sections, but the views make it worth the effort. The sight of the glacier at the end is unforgettable.

3. Iceberg Lake Trail

- **Location:** Many Glacier Area

- **Trail Length:** 9.7 miles (15.6 kilometers) round trip
- **Elevation Gain:** 1,200 feet (366 meters)
- **Difficulty:** Moderate
- **Parking:** Free, at Swiftcurrent Motor Inn
- **Highlights:** Alpine lake, wildflowers, dramatic scenery

The Iceberg Lake Trail is another favorite in the Many Glacier area, known for its beautiful scenery and the striking blue lake at the end, often filled with floating icebergs even in summer. The hike is moderately difficult, with a steady climb that rewards you with stunning views of the surrounding peaks and wildflower-filled meadows.

Challenging Hikes

For experienced hikers looking for a real challenge, these strenuous hikes offer incredible rewards in terms of scenery and accomplishment.

1. Ptarmigan Tunnel

- **Location:** Many Glacier Area
- **Trail Length:** 10.6 miles (17.1 kilometers) round trip
- **Elevation Gain:** 2,300 feet (701 meters)

- **Difficulty:** Strenuous
- **Parking:** Free, at Swiftcurrent Motor Inn
- **Highlights:** Tunnel through the mountain, panoramic views, wildlife

The Ptarmigan Tunnel hike is a tough trail that takes you through lush forests and alpine meadows before reaching a tunnel carved through the mountain in the 1930s. On the other side, you'll find stunning views of the Belly River and the remote wilderness beyond.

2. Siyeh Pass Trail

- **Location:** Starts at Siyeh Bend, along the Going-to-the-Sun Road

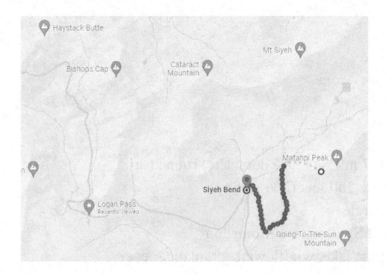

- **Trail Length:** 10.3 miles (16.6 kilometers) round trip
- **Elevation Gain:** 2,240 feet (683 meters)
- **Difficulty:** Strenuous
- **Parking:** Free, at Siyeh Bend
- **Highlights:** Panoramic views, wildflowers, diverse ecosystems

The Siyeh Pass Trail is one of the park's top hikes, taking you through different landscapes, from dense forests to high alpine meadows. The trail ends at Siyeh Pass, offering incredible views of the surrounding peaks and valleys. It's a tough hike with significant elevation gain, but the views are some of the best in the park.

3. Gunsight Pass

- **Location:** Starts at Jackson Glacier Overlook, Going-to-the-Sun Road
- **Trail Length:** 20 miles (32.2 kilometers) point-to-point

- **Elevation Gain:** 3,400 feet (1,036 meters)
- **Difficulty:** Strenuous
- **Parking:** Free, at Jackson Glacier Overlook or Lake McDonald Lodge (shuttle recommended)
- **Highlights:** Glacier views, alpine lakes, diverse ecosystems

Gunsight Pass is one of the most challenging hikes in Glacier National Park, offering a true backcountry experience. This long and strenuous trail takes you over Gunsight Pass, with incredible views of the park's glaciers, lakes, and mountains. The hike can be done as a very long day hike, but it's more commonly completed as an overnight backpacking trip.

Essential Hiking Tips and Safety

Hiking in Glacier National Park can be an unforgettable experience, but it's important to be prepared and follow safety guidelines to ensure a safe and enjoyable trip.

1. Plan Ahead and Be Prepared

- **Weather:** Glacier's weather can change rapidly, especially at higher elevations. Always check the forecast before heading out and be prepared for sudden changes.
- **Gear:** Wear sturdy, broken-in hiking boots and dress in layers to adapt to changing temperatures. Always carry a map, compass, or GPS, and know how to use them.
- **Water and Food:** Bring plenty of water and high-energy snacks. There are few opportunities to refill water on most trails, so plan accordingly.

2. Wildlife Safety

- **Bear Safety:** Glacier is home to both black bears and grizzly bears. Carry bear spray and know how to use it. Make noise while hiking, especially in dense vegetation or near streams where bears might be harder to see.
- **Other Wildlife:** Keep a safe distance from all wildlife, including mountain goats, bighorn sheep, and moose. Never approach or feed animals.

3. Trail Etiquette

- **Leave No Trace:** Pack out all trash and minimize your impact on the environment. Stay on marked trails to protect the fragile ecosystems.

- **Yield to Others:** Uphill hikers have the right of way. Step aside on narrow trails to allow them to pass.

4. Know Your Limits

- **Choose the Right Trail:** Be honest about your fitness level and choose a trail that matches your abilities. It's better to start with easier hikes and work your way up to more challenging trails.
- **Pace Yourself:** Take your time and enjoy the journey. Rest when needed and don't push yourself too hard, especially at higher elevations.

5. Emergencies

- **First Aid:** Carry a basic first aid kit and know how to treat common hiking injuries like blisters, sprains, and cuts.
- **Communication:** Cell service is limited in the park. Consider carrying a satellite communication device if you're heading into remote areas.

Flora and Fauna: What to Expect

Glacier National Park is home to a wide variety of plants and animals, many of which you're likely to encounter on the trails.

1. Flora

- **Wildflowers:** Glacier's alpine meadows are famous for their wildflower displays, especially in mid to late summer. Look for Indian paintbrush, lupine, and beargrass, among others.
- **Forests:** Lower elevations are covered in dense forests of western red cedar, hemlock, and lodgepole pine. As you climb higher, these give way to subalpine fir and Engelmann spruce.

2. Fauna

- **Mammals:** The park is home to a variety of mammals, including grizzly and black bears, mountain goats, bighorn sheep, elk, and moose. Smaller mammals like marmots, pikas, and squirrels are also common.
- **Birds:** Birdwatchers will enjoy spotting species like the Clark's nutcracker, golden eagle, and various woodpeckers and warblers.
- **Insects:** In summer, be prepared for mosquitoes and biting flies, especially near water. Carry insect repellent to help keep them at bay.

Wildlife Viewing in Glacier National Park

Glacier National Park is one of the premier destinations in North America for wildlife viewing. With its vast and diverse habitats, ranging from alpine meadows to dense forests and glacial lakes, the park is home to a rich variety of animal species. Whether you're an experienced wildlife enthusiast or a casual observer, Glacier offers numerous opportunities to see animals in their natural environment. This chapter will guide you through the common wildlife species in the park, the best spots for viewing them, and essential safety tips to ensure a safe and enjoyable experience.

Common Wildlife Species

1. Grizzly Bears and Black Bears

Grizzly bears and black bears are two of the most iconic species in Glacier National Park. Both species are commonly seen throughout the park, though they prefer different habitats.

- **Grizzly Bears:** Grizzlies are larger and have a distinct hump on their shoulders, which differentiates them from black bears. These bears are usually found in open meadows, along rivers, and in higher elevations where they forage for roots, berries, and small mammals. Grizzlies are solitary animals and are more commonly seen in the early morning or late evening when they are most active.
- **Black Bears:** Black bears, which can range in color from black to brown, are smaller than grizzlies and are often found in forested areas where they feed on berries, nuts, and insects. Unlike grizzlies, black bears are more likely to climb trees when threatened. They are also more adaptable and can be found in a wider range of habitats throughout the park.

2. Mountain Goats

Mountain goats are perhaps the most iconic animals in Glacier National Park. These sure-footed creatures are commonly seen on the park's rugged cliffs and steep slopes. With their thick white coats and sharp black horns, mountain goats are well adapted to the cold, mountainous environments. They are often spotted near Logan Pass and along the Highline Trail, where they can be seen grazing on grasses and shrubs.

3. Bighorn Sheep

Bighorn sheep are another common sight in Glacier, particularly in areas like Many Glacier and the Logan Pass region. These animals are known for their impressive, curved horns and their ability to navigate steep, rocky terrain. Bighorn sheep are often seen in large groups, especially during the summer and fall when they come down to lower elevations to graze.

4. Elk and Moose

Elk and moose are two of the largest mammals in Glacier National Park. Elk are commonly found in the park's meadows and forests, especially during the fall rutting season when the males bugle to attract females. Moose, on the other hand, prefer wetter habitats and are often seen near lakes, rivers, and marshy areas. Moose are solitary animals and are best spotted during the early morning or late evening.

Best Spots for Wildlife Viewing

Glacier National Park offers many excellent spots for wildlife viewing. Some areas are particularly known for their abundance of specific species.

1. Logan Pass

- **Location:** Along the Going-to-the-Sun Road
- **Best Time to Visit:** Early morning or late evening

Logan Pass is one of the most popular spots for wildlife viewing in Glacier. The high elevation and open meadows make it an ideal location for spotting mountain goats, bighorn sheep, and occasionally grizzly bears. The nearby Highline Trail and Hidden Lake Trail are excellent for observing wildlife in their natural habitats.

2. Many Glacier

- **Location:** Northeastern Glacier National Park
- **Best Time to Visit:** Early morning or dusk

Many Glacier is often considered the best area in the park for wildlife viewing. The region's diverse habitats, including forests, meadows, and lakes, support a wide range of animals. Grizzly bears, black bears, moose, and bighorn sheep are commonly seen here. The trails around Swiftcurrent Lake and Grinnell Glacier are particularly good for wildlife spotting.

3. Two Medicine

- **Location:** Southeastern Glacier National Park
- **Best Time to Visit:** Morning or late afternoon

The Two Medicine area is less crowded than other parts of the park, making it a great spot for observing wildlife in a quieter setting. Moose are frequently seen near the lake, especially in the early morning. Bighorn sheep and black bears are also common in this area.

4. St. Mary Valley

- **Location:** Eastern Glacier National Park
- **Best Time to Visit:** Early morning or late evening

St. Mary Valley is another prime location for wildlife viewing. The valley's diverse ecosystems provide habitat for grizzly bears, black bears, elk, and mountain goats. The area around St. Mary Lake and the Going-to-the-Sun Road offers several excellent viewpoints for observing these animals.

5. North Fork

- **Location:** Northwestern Glacier National Park
- **Best Time to Visit:** Anytime during the day

The North Fork area is one of the more remote regions of Glacier National Park, offering a more wilderness-oriented experience. This area is known for its grizzly bear population, and visitors might also spot black bears, elk, and wolves. The fewer crowds make it a great place for those looking to see wildlife in a more natural setting.

Safety Tips for Wildlife Encounters

Encountering wildlife in Glacier National Park can be thrilling, but it's important to remember that these are wild animals and should be treated with respect. Here are some essential safety tips to keep in mind:

1. Keep Your Distance

Always observe wildlife from a safe distance. For bears, this means staying at least 100 yards away. For other animals like moose, elk, and bighorn sheep, maintain a distance of at least 25 yards. Never approach or attempt to feed any wild animals.

2. Be Bear Aware

Glacier National Park is bear country, so it's crucial to be bear-aware. Carry bear spray and know how to use it. Make noise while hiking, especially in dense vegetation or near streams, to avoid surprising a bear. If you do encounter a bear, stay calm, back away slowly, and do not run.

3. Stay on Marked Trails

Staying on marked trails not only helps protect the park's fragile ecosystems but also reduces your chances of surprising wildlife. Animals are more likely to avoid areas with regular human activity, so sticking to trails is safer.

4. Hike in Groups

Hiking in groups is safer than hiking alone, as groups are less likely to surprise wildlife. If you're hiking in bear country, make sure everyone in your group is aware of bear safety practices.

5. Store Food Properly

When camping, always store your food and scented items in bear-proof containers or hang them from a tree, following the park's guidelines. This helps prevent bears from becoming habituated to human food, which can lead to dangerous situations.

6. Respect Wildlife

Respect wildlife by not disturbing them. Keep noise levels down when near animals and never try to attract their attention. Remember that you are a guest in their home.

Birdwatching in Glacier National Park

Glacier National Park is also a fantastic destination for birdwatchers. With over 270 species recorded in the park, birdwatchers can enjoy spotting a wide variety of birds, from common species to more elusive ones.

1. Common Bird Species

- **Clark's Nutcracker:** Often seen in the park's higher elevations, especially around Logan Pass. These birds are known for their distinctive calls and are often spotted in alpine meadows and forests.
- **Golden Eagle:** These majestic birds of prey can be seen soaring high above the park's mountains and valleys. They are more commonly spotted in remote areas like the North Fork and Many Glacier.
- **Mountain Bluebird:** A beautiful bird with bright blue feathers, often seen in open meadows and along the park's trails.
- **American Dipper:** This small bird is commonly seen near rivers and streams, where it dives underwater in search of food.

2. Best Birdwatching Spots

- **Swiftcurrent Lake:** Located in Many Glacier, this area is excellent for spotting a variety of bird species, especially waterfowl and raptors.
- **St. Mary Lake:** The eastern side of the park is home to a diverse range of bird species, and St. Mary Lake offers great opportunities to see them, especially in the early morning.
- **Two Medicine Lake:** This area is quieter than other parts of the park, making it a good spot for birdwatching without the crowds.

3. Birdwatching Tips

- **Bring Binoculars:** A good pair of binoculars is essential for birdwatching, allowing you to see birds from a distance without disturbing them.
- **Go Early:** Birds are most active in the early morning, so plan your birdwatching outings for just after sunrise.
- **Be Patient:** Birdwatching requires patience. Find a quiet spot, sit down, and wait for the birds to come to you.

Camping and Lodging in Glacier National Park

Glacier National Park offers a range of camping and lodging options, making it possible for visitors to experience the park's beauty in a way that best suits their preferences. Whether you prefer the convenience of a frontcountry campground, the adventure of backcountry camping, or the comfort of a historic lodge, Glacier has something to offer. This chapter provides an in-depth look at the various options available for staying in and around the park, including locations, pricing, and key points to consider when planning your trip.

Overview of Camping Options

Glacier National Park offers two main types of camping experiences: frontcountry and backcountry camping. Frontcountry campgrounds are accessible by vehicle and offer amenities such as restrooms and potable water, making them a convenient option for most visitors. Backcountry camping, on the other hand, is for those seeking a more rugged and remote experience, requiring a hike to reach the campsites.

Frontcountry Campgrounds

Glacier National Park has 13 frontcountry campgrounds, providing over 1,000 campsites. These campgrounds are spread throughout the park, offering a range of environments and proximity to key attractions. Some campgrounds are first-come, first-served, while others accept reservations.

1. Apgar Campground

- **Location:** Near West Glacier Entrance
- **Number of Sites:** 194
- **Pricing:** $20 per night
- **Reservations:** Available for some sites through Recreation.gov
- **Amenities:** Potable water, restrooms, picnic tables, fire rings, RV dump station

Apgar Campground is the largest and most popular campground in Glacier National Park. Located near the West Glacier Entrance, it offers easy access to Lake McDonald, the Apgar Visitor Center, and the Going-to-the-Sun Road. The campground is suitable for tents and RVs, with some sites available for reservation.

2. Many Glacier Campground

- **Location:** Many Glacier Area
- **Number of Sites:** 109
- **Pricing:** $23 per night

- **Reservations:** Required for most sites during peak season
- **Amenities:** Potable water, restrooms, picnic tables, fire rings, food storage lockers

Many Glacier Campground is one of the most scenic and sought-after campgrounds in the park, located in the heart of the Many Glacier Valley. This area is known for its stunning landscapes and abundant wildlife. The campground is close to popular hiking trails, such as the Grinnell Glacier Trail and Iceberg Lake Trail.

3. St. Mary Campground

- **Location:** Near St. Mary Entrance
- **Number of Sites:** 148
- **Pricing:** $20 per night
- **Reservations:** Available through Recreation.gov
- **Amenities:** Potable water, restrooms, picnic tables, fire rings, RV dump station

St. Mary Campground is the largest campground on the east side of the park, located near the St. Mary Entrance and the beginning of the Going-to-the-Sun Road. This campground provides easy access to the St. Mary Visitor Center, St. Mary Lake, and several popular hiking trails.

Backcountry Camping

For those looking to experience Glacier National Park's wilderness more intimately, backcountry camping is an excellent option. Backcountry campsites are located far from roads and require a hike to reach. These sites offer a secluded and immersive experience in nature but require more planning and preparation.

Permits and Reservations

Backcountry camping in Glacier National Park requires a permit, which can be obtained through a lottery system, by advance reservation, or on a walk-in basis. Permits are essential to ensure that the wilderness is preserved and that the number of visitors is managed to reduce environmental impact.

- **Pricing:** $10 per trip, plus $7 per person per night
- **Reservations:** Available through Recreation.gov, with a portion of permits reserved for walk-ins on a first-come, first-served basis

Popular Backcountry Campsites

Glacier National Park has dozens of designated backcountry campsites, each offering unique views and experiences. Here are some of the most popular ones:

1. Granite Park Chalet Area

- **Location:** Near the end of the Highline Trail
- **Highlights:** Stunning views, proximity to Granite Park Chalet
- **Access:** Hike-in only

The Granite Park area is a popular destination for backcountry hikers, offering stunning views of the surrounding peaks and valleys. The nearby Granite Park Chalet provides a unique experience where hikers can enjoy rustic accommodations and meals in the backcountry, though reservations for the chalet itself are separate.

2. Kootenai Lakes

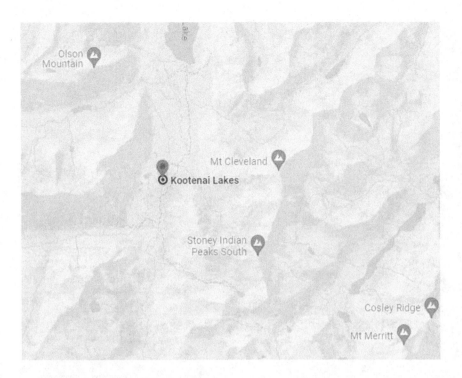

- **Location:** North Fork Area
- **Highlights:** Remote location, excellent wildlife viewing
- **Access:** Hike-in only

Kootenai Lakes is one of the more remote backcountry campsites, located in the less-visited North Fork area of the park. The site is known for its tranquility and excellent opportunities to see wildlife, including moose and beavers.

3. Sperry Chalet Area

- **Location:** Near Sperry Glacier
- **Highlights:** Historic chalet, access to Sperry Glacier
- **Access:** Hike-in only

The Sperry Chalet area offers a mix of backcountry camping and historic charm. The nearby Sperry Chalet, which was rebuilt after a fire, offers rustic lodging, while the campsite itself provides access to some of the park's more rugged and scenic areas, including Sperry Glacier.

Lodges and Hotels Inside the Park

For those who prefer the comfort of a bed and the amenities of a hotel, Glacier National Park offers several historic lodges and inns. These accommodations provide a unique opportunity to stay within the park and experience its beauty up close.

1. Lake McDonald Lodge

- **Location:** West side of the park, along Going-to-the-Sun Road

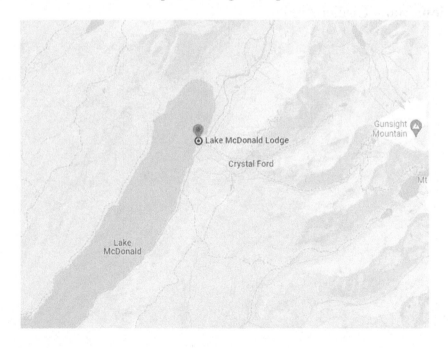

- **Pricing:** $200 to $450 per night, depending on the season and room type
- **Amenities:** Restaurant, lounge, gift shop, boat tours, Wi-Fi

Lake McDonald Lodge is one of the most iconic lodges in Glacier National Park. Built in 1913, this historic lodge offers stunning views of Lake McDonald and easy access to the park's main attractions. The lodge features a rustic design with a grand lobby, cozy rooms, and a lakeside restaurant.

2. Many Glacier Hotel

- **Location:** Many Glacier Area

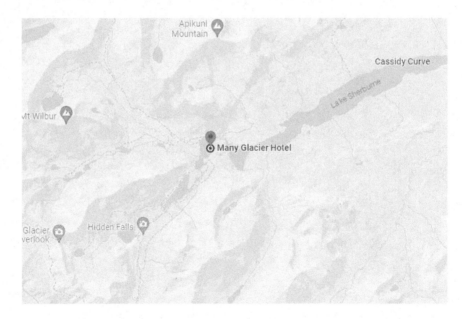

- **Pricing:** $250 to $500 per night, depending on the season and room type
- **Amenities:** Restaurant, lounge, gift shop, boat tours, Wi-Fi

Many Glacier Hotel is often referred to as the "Gem of the West" and is one of the most picturesque lodges in the park. Located on the shores of Swiftcurrent Lake, the hotel offers stunning views of the surrounding mountains and easy access to popular hiking trails.

3. Rising Sun Motor Inn

- **Location:** Near St. Mary, along the Going-to-the-Sun Road

- **Pricing:** $150 to $300 per night, depending on the season and room type
- **Amenities:** Restaurant, gift shop, Wi-Fi

Rising Sun Motor Inn offers a more modest lodging option within the park. Located near St. Mary, this motor inn provides a convenient base for exploring the eastern side of Glacier, including St. Mary Lake and the Going-to-the-Sun Road.

Lodging Outside the Park

If the park's lodges are fully booked or if you prefer staying outside the park, there are numerous accommodations in the nearby towns of West Glacier, St. Mary, and East Glacier. These towns offer a range of options, from budget motels to luxury resorts.

1. West Glacier Accommodations

- **Location:** Near the West Glacier Entrance
- **Pricing:** $100 to $400 per night, depending on the type of accommodation and season
- **Options:** Hotels, motels, cabins, vacation rentals

West Glacier is the gateway to the park's west side and offers a variety of lodging options. This area is ideal for those looking to stay close to the park's main entrance while enjoying additional amenities like dining and shopping.

2. St. Mary and East Glacier Options

- **Location:** Near the St. Mary and East Glacier Entrances
- **Pricing:** $100 to $300 per night, depending on the type of accommodation and season
- **Options:** Hotels, motels, lodges, vacation rentals

St. Mary and East Glacier provide excellent options for those wishing to explore the park's eastern side. St. Mary is closer to the Going-to-the-Sun Road and offers easy access to St. Mary Lake and other eastern attractions. East Glacier is slightly farther but offers a more relaxed, small-town atmosphere.

RV Camping and Services

For visitors traveling with an RV, Glacier National Park and its surrounding areas offer several campgrounds and RV parks equipped with the necessary amenities.

1. Apgar Campground

- **Location:** Near the West Glacier Entrance
- **Pricing:** $20 per night
- **Amenities:** RV dump station, potable water, restrooms, picnic tables

Apgar Campground is one of the few campgrounds within the park that can accommodate RVs. It's a popular choice due to its location near Lake McDonald and its proximity to the Going-to-the-Sun Road. The campground has a dump station and potable water, but it does not offer electrical hookups.

2. St. Mary Campground

- **Location:** Near the St. Mary Entrance
- **Pricing:** $20 per night
- **Amenities:** RV dump station, potable water, restrooms, picnic tables

St. Mary Campground is another good option for RV camping, located near the St. Mary Entrance on the east side of the park. Like Apgar, it provides basic services for RVs but no electrical hookups.

3. Private RV Parks

- **Location:** West Glacier, St. Mary, East Glacier
- **Pricing:** $40 to $80 per night, depending on the park and season
- **Amenities:** Full hookups, Wi-Fi, showers, laundry facilities

Outside the park, several private RV parks offer full hookups and additional amenities such as Wi-Fi, showers, and laundry facilities. These parks are located in West Glacier, St. Mary, and East Glacier, providing convenient access to the park's entrances.

Activities and Adventures

Glacier National Park offers a wide range of activities and adventures for visitors of all ages and interests. Whether you're looking to explore the park's stunning landscapes through guided tours, engage in outdoor sports like boating and fishing, or capture the park's beauty through photography, Glacier has something for everyone. This chapter provides an overview of some of the most popular activities available in the park, including locations, pricing, and key points to help you plan your visit.

Guided Tours and Ranger Programs

Guided tours and ranger programs are a great way to learn more about Glacier National Park's natural and cultural history. These programs offer insight into the park's unique geology, wildlife, and ecosystems, all led by knowledgeable guides or park rangers.

1. Red Bus Tours

- **Location:** Depart from various locations, including Apgar Visitor Center, Lake McDonald Lodge, and Many Glacier Hotel
- **Pricing:** $70 to $100 per person, depending on the tour length
- **Duration:** 3 to 9 hours, depending on the tour

Red Bus Tours are a popular way to see Glacier National Park, offering guided tours in historic open-top buses. These tours take you along the Going-to-the-Sun Road and other scenic routes, with stops at key points of interest. The drivers, known as "jammers," provide commentary on the park's history, geology, and wildlife.

2. Ranger-Led Programs

- **Location:** Various locations throughout the park, including visitor centers, campgrounds, and popular trailheads
- **Pricing:** Free with park admission

- **Duration:** 1 to 2 hours, depending on the program

Ranger-led programs are offered throughout Glacier National Park and cover a wide range of topics, including wildlife, geology, and cultural history. These programs include guided hikes, evening talks at campgrounds, and educational programs for children.

Boating and Fishing

Glacier National Park's pristine lakes and rivers provide excellent opportunities for boating and fishing. Whether you're looking to paddle on a calm lake or cast a line in a trout-filled stream, Glacier has something to offer water enthusiasts.

1. Boating

- **Location:** Popular lakes for boating include Lake McDonald, Two Medicine Lake, and St. Mary Lake
- **Pricing:** Boat rentals range from $15 to $30 per hour, depending on the type of boat
- **Availability:** Rentals available at Apgar Village, Two Medicine, and Rising Sun

Boating is a popular activity on Glacier's lakes, offering a peaceful way to enjoy the park's scenery from the water. Canoes, kayaks, rowboats, and motorboats are available for rent at several locations throughout the park. Visitors can also bring their own non-motorized boats, but they must be inspected for aquatic invasive species before launching.

2. Fishing

- **Location:** Lakes and rivers throughout the park, including Lake McDonald, Two Medicine Lake, and the Flathead River
- **Pricing:** Free with a valid Montana fishing license; no park-specific permit required
- **Regulations:** Follow Montana state fishing regulations

Fishing in Glacier National Park offers anglers the chance to catch a variety of fish, including cutthroat trout, rainbow trout, and brook trout. No additional permit is required beyond a Montana fishing license, and fishing is allowed in most of the park's waters. Popular spots include Lake McDonald, Two Medicine Lake, and various rivers and streams throughout the park.

Horseback Riding

Horseback riding is a classic way to explore Glacier National Park, offering a chance to see the park's landscapes from a different perspective. Guided horseback rides are available through several concessionaires within the park.

1. Swan Mountain Outfitters

- **Location:** Rides depart from Apgar, Lake McDonald, and Many Glacier
- **Pricing:** $60 to $225 per person, depending on the ride length
- **Duration:** 1 hour to full-day rides available

Swan Mountain Outfitters offers guided horseback rides throughout Glacier National Park. These rides vary in length from one-hour introductory rides to full-day adventures, taking visitors through forests, along lakes, and to scenic overlooks. The outfitters provide well-trained horses and experienced guides, making this activity accessible even for beginners.

Photography Hotspots

Glacier National Park is a photographer's paradise, with stunning landscapes and abundant wildlife providing endless opportunities for capturing memorable images. Some locations are particularly renowned for their photogenic qualities.

1. Wild Goose Island

- **Location:** St. Mary Lake, along the Going-to-the-Sun Road
- **Best Time:** Sunrise or sunset

Wild Goose Island, located in St. Mary Lake, is one of the most photographed spots in Glacier National Park. The small island, set against the backdrop of the towering peaks of the Continental Divide, is especially beautiful at sunrise or sunset when the light is soft and golden.

2. Logan Pass

- **Location:** Along the Going-to-the-Sun Road
- **Best Time:** Early morning or late afternoon

Logan Pass, the highest point on the Going-to-the-Sun Road, offers stunning panoramic views of the surrounding mountains and valleys. The area is also known for its wildflowers and wildlife, making it a favorite spot for photographers.

Winter Activities: Snowshoeing and Cross-Country Skiing

While Glacier National Park is best known for its summer activities, winter offers a quieter, snow-covered landscape perfect for snowshoeing and cross-country skiing.

1. Snowshoeing

- **Location:** Apgar, Lake McDonald, and Marias Pass
- **Pricing:** Free if you bring your own snowshoes; rentals available in nearby towns for $10 to $20 per day

Snowshoeing is a great way to explore Glacier's winter wonderland. The park offers several trails suitable for snowshoeing, including areas around Apgar and Lake McDonald. Guided snowshoe walks are sometimes offered by the park in winter, providing a chance to learn about winter ecology.

Key Points:

- **Quiet Beauty:** Winter offers a peaceful, crowd-free experience in the park.
- **Accessible for All:** Snowshoeing is easy to learn and accessible for all fitness levels.

2. Cross-Country Skiing

- **Location:** Trails near Apgar, Lake McDonald, and along the Camas Road
- **Pricing:** Free if you bring your own skis; rentals available in nearby towns for $15 to $25 per day

Cross-country skiing is another popular winter activity in Glacier. The park has several groomed and ungroomed trails that are ideal for skiing, offering a unique way to see Glacier's snowy landscapes.

Key Points:

- **Winter Adventure:** Cross-country skiing allows you to cover more ground and explore deeper into the park during the winter months.
- **Variety of Trails:** From easy routes near Apgar to more challenging terrain, there's something for every skier.

Family-Friendly Activities

Glacier National Park is a fantastic destination for families, offering a variety of activities that are both fun and educational for children of all ages.

1. Junior Ranger Program

- **Location:** Available at all visitor centers
- **Pricing:** Free with park admission

The Junior Ranger Program is a popular activity for children visiting Glacier National Park. Kids can pick up a Junior Ranger booklet at any visitor center, complete the activities, and earn a Junior Ranger badge. The program is designed to educate children about the park's natural and cultural resources in a fun, interactive way.

2. Apgar Nature Center

- **Location:** Apgar Village

- **Pricing:** Free with park admission

The Apgar Nature Center offers hands-on exhibits and activities designed for children. It's a great place for families to learn about the park's wildlife, plants, and ecosystems in an interactive setting.

Cultural and Historical Sites

Glacier National Park is not only a place of immense natural beauty but also a region rich in cultural and historical significance. The park's history is intertwined with the legacy of Native American tribes, the influence of the Great Northern Railway, and the development of historic lodges and chalets that have become iconic landmarks. This chapter explores the cultural and historical sites within Glacier National Park and nearby areas, providing insights into the park's heritage, visitor centers, dining options, and surrounding attractions.

Native American Heritage

Glacier National Park is located on lands that have been inhabited by Native American tribes for thousands of years. The Blackfeet, Salish, Kootenai, and Pend d'Oreille tribes have deep cultural and spiritual connections to the land that is now part of the park. Their traditions, stories, and practices are an integral part of the park's history and continue to influence its stewardship and interpretation.

1. Blackfeet Nation

- **Location:** East side of Glacier National Park
- **Pricing:** Entry to Blackfeet Nation events and cultural sites may vary; check with local tribal offices for details.

The Blackfeet Nation, or Amskapi Piikani, has lived in the plains east of the Rocky Mountains for centuries. Their territory includes the eastern portion of what is now Glacier National Park. The Blackfeet people consider this area sacred, referring to it as the "Backbone of the World." Visitors can explore Blackfeet culture through guided tours, powwows, and museums on the Blackfeet Reservation, just outside the park's boundaries.

2. Salish, Kootenai, and Pend d'Oreille Tribes

- **Location:** Flathead Indian Reservation, south of Glacier National Park
- **Pricing:** Entry to cultural sites and events may vary; check with local tribal offices for details.

The Salish, Kootenai, and Pend d'Oreille tribes have historically lived in the areas surrounding Glacier National Park, particularly in the Flathead Valley. The tribes were known for their extensive knowledge of the land, including hunting, fishing, and gathering practices. Today, the Flathead Indian Reservation is home to the Confederated Salish and Kootenai Tribes, who continue to preserve and promote their cultural heritage.

3. The Native America Speaks Program

- **Location:** Various locations within Glacier National Park, including Apgar Amphitheater, Many Glacier, and St. Mary Visitor Center
- **Pricing:** Free with park admission

The Native America Speaks program is a long-standing series of presentations and performances held in Glacier National Park. The program features tribal members from the Blackfeet, Salish, Kootenai, and Pend d'Oreille tribes who share their cultures through storytelling, music, and dance. These presentations offer visitors a deeper understanding of the park's significance to Native American people.

Historic Chalets and Lodges

Glacier National Park is home to several historic chalets and lodges that were built in the early 20th century, primarily by the Great Northern Railway. These structures were designed to blend with the natural surroundings and provide visitors with comfortable accommodations in remote and scenic locations. Many of these buildings have been preserved and continue to operate as lodges and museums, offering a glimpse into the park's early tourism history.

1. Lake McDonald Lodge

- **Location:** West side of Glacier National Park, along Going-to-the-Sun Road
- **Pricing:** Rooms range from $200 to $450 per night, depending on the season and room type

Lake McDonald Lodge is one of the most iconic lodges in Glacier National Park. Built in 1913, the lodge is located on the shores of Lake McDonald and is designed in the Swiss-chalet style, reflecting the influence of the Great Northern Railway's marketing of the park as the "American Alps." The lodge features a grand lobby with a massive stone fireplace, rustic woodwork, and animal mounts, creating an atmosphere of early 20th-century wilderness luxury.

2. Many Glacier Hotel

- **Location:** Many Glacier Valley, northeastern Glacier National Park
- **Pricing:** Rooms range from $250 to $500 per night, depending on the season and room type

Many Glacier Hotel, often referred to as the "Gem of the West," is another historic lodge built by the Great Northern Railway. Located on the shores of Swiftcurrent Lake, the hotel offers breathtaking views of the surrounding mountains and is a gateway to some of the park's most popular hiking trails. The hotel was constructed in 1915 and features a timber-framed lobby, large stone fireplace, and Swiss-inspired architecture.

3. Sperry Chalet

- **Location:** Near Sperry Glacier, accessible by trail from Lake McDonald Lodge
- **Pricing:** Rates start at $245 per person per night, including meals

Sperry Chalet is one of the few remaining backcountry lodges in Glacier National Park. Built in 1913 by the Great Northern Railway, the chalet is located high in the mountains, offering a remote and rugged experience for hikers. Sperry Chalet was heavily damaged by a fire in 2017 but has since been restored and reopened to the public. Guests can stay overnight in the chalet, with meals provided by the chalet's staff.

4. Granite Park Chalet

- **Location:** Along the Highline Trail, accessible from Logan Pass
- **Pricing:** Rates start at $110 per person per night, no meals included (guests must bring their own food)

Granite Park Chalet is another backcountry lodge in Glacier National Park, offering rustic accommodations for hikers along the Highline Trail. Built in 1914 by the Great Northern Railway, the chalet provides basic accommodations in a remote setting, with stunning views of the surrounding mountains. Unlike Sperry Chalet, Granite Park Chalet does not provide meals, so guests must bring their own food and prepare it in the chalet's kitchen.

The Great Northern Railway and Glacier

The development of Glacier National Park is closely linked to the history of the Great Northern Railway, which played a significant role in promoting the park as a tourist destination. The railway built many of the park's iconic lodges and chalets and helped shape the early tourism industry in the region.

1. The Influence of the Great Northern Railway

- **Location:** Throughout Glacier National Park
- **Pricing:** Varies depending on the specific sites and tours

The Great Northern Railway, led by entrepreneur James J. Hill, was instrumental in the creation and promotion of Glacier National Park. The railway's marketing efforts, including the construction of lodges and chalets, were designed to attract wealthy tourists to the park, positioning Glacier as the "American Alps." The railway also played a key role in the establishment of the park itself, lobbying for its designation as a national park in 1910.

2. Great Northern Railway Buildings

- **Location:** Various locations within Glacier National Park
- **Pricing:** Varies depending on the specific buildings and tours

Many of Glacier's most famous buildings were constructed by the Great Northern Railway, including the lodges, chalets, and even the park's early visitor centers. These structures were designed to blend with the natural surroundings, using local materials and architecture inspired by the Swiss Alps. The emphasis on rustic elegance helped establish Glacier National Park as a premier destination for luxury tourism in the early 20th century.

3. The Empire Builder Train

- **Location:** Amtrak's Empire Builder Route, with stops in East Glacier Park, Essex, and West Glacier
- **Pricing:** Ticket prices vary depending on the season, distance traveled, and type of accommodation; prices range from $50 for a short segment to over $1,000 for a sleeper cabin on longer journeys

Amtrak's Empire Builder is a direct descendant of the original Great Northern Railway trains that brought visitors to Glacier National Park. The Empire Builder runs from Chicago to Seattle and Portland, passing through Glacier National Park along the way. The train offers stunning views of the park's scenery and stops at several locations near the park's entrances.

Museums and Visitor Centers

Glacier National Park's visitor centers and museums provide excellent resources for learning about the park's natural and cultural history. These centers offer exhibits, educational programs, and essential information for planning your visit.

1. Apgar Visitor Center

- **Location:** Near the West Glacier Entrance
- **Pricing:** Free with park admission

The Apgar Visitor Center is the primary visitor center on the west side of Glacier National Park. It offers a range of exhibits on the park's geology, wildlife, and history, as well as maps, guides, and information on current conditions. The center also serves as a starting point for ranger-led programs and the Native America Speaks presentations.

2. Logan Pass Visitor Center

- **Location:** Along the Going-to-the-Sun Road, at the highest point on the road
- **Pricing:** Free with park admission

The Logan Pass Visitor Center is located at the highest point along the Going-to-the-Sun Road, offering stunning views and access to some of the park's most popular trails, including the Hidden Lake Trail and the Highline Trail. The visitor center features exhibits on the park's alpine environment and the impact of climate change on the glaciers. It's also a hub for ranger-led hikes and programs.

3. Many Glacier Hotel's History Room

- **Location:** Inside Many Glacier Hotel, Many Glacier Valley
- **Pricing:** Free with park admission

The History Room at Many Glacier Hotel is dedicated to the rich history of the hotel and its role in the development of Glacier National Park. The room features historical photographs, artifacts, and exhibits that tell the story of the hotel's construction, its early guests, and the role of the Great Northern Railway in promoting the park.

Dining and Shopping

Glacier National Park is not only a destination for breathtaking scenery and outdoor adventure, but it also offers visitors a delightful range of dining and shopping experiences. Whether you're looking to enjoy a meal surrounded by nature, stock up on supplies for your adventures, or bring home a piece of the park through unique souvenirs, Glacier has something for everyone. This chapter provides a comprehensive guide to dining and shopping options within and around the park, including locations, pricing, and recommendations for must-try dishes and unique finds.

Dining Inside the Park

One of the best ways to immerse yourself in the beauty of Glacier National Park is by enjoying a meal within its boundaries. The park offers a variety of dining options, ranging from casual eateries to more refined establishments. Many of these dining spots are located within the historic lodges, providing both a sense of history and a taste of local flavors.

Restaurants and Cafes

1. **Lake McDonald Lodge**
   - **Location**: West Glacier, Lake McDonald Lodge
   - **Cuisine**: American, with a focus on local and seasonal ingredients
   - **Pricing**: Entrees range from $15 to $30
   - **Details**: The Lake McDonald Lodge, one of the most iconic lodges in the park, offers several dining options. The main dining room, Russell's Fireside Dining Room, provides a warm and inviting atmosphere with large windows overlooking Lake McDonald. Here, you can enjoy dishes such as bison meatloaf, grilled Montana trout, and huckleberry desserts, all made with local ingredients. The lodge also features Jammer Joe's Grill and Pizzeria, offering a more casual menu including pizzas, burgers, and sandwiches, with prices ranging from $10 to $20.

2. **Many Glacier Hotel**
   - **Location**: Many Glacier Valley
   - **Cuisine**: American, featuring regional specialties
   - **Pricing**: Entrees range from $20 to $40
   - **Details**: The Ptarmigan Dining Room at Many Glacier Hotel offers spectacular views of Swiftcurrent Lake and the surrounding peaks. The menu highlights regional cuisine, including dishes like Montana-raised beef, elk medallions, and fresh lake fish. The hotel's Swiss Lounge offers lighter fare and a selection of local craft beers, with prices for small plates and sandwiches ranging from $10 to $20.

3. **Two Dog Flats Grill**
   - **Location**: Rising Sun Motor Inn
   - **Cuisine**: American, casual dining
   - **Pricing**: Entrees range from $12 to $25
   - **Details**: Located near St. Mary Lake, Two Dog Flats Grill offers a more casual dining experience with a focus on comfort food. The menu includes

favorites like bison burgers, roasted chicken, and hearty salads. It's a great spot to grab a quick bite before heading out for a day of exploring.

4. **Belton Chalet**
   - **Location**: West Glacier
   - **Cuisine**: American, fine dining
   - **Pricing**: Entrees range from $25 to $50
   - **Details**: Just outside the park's west entrance, the Belton Chalet offers a fine dining experience in a historic setting. The menu changes seasonally, but you can expect dishes like cedar-plank salmon, duck breast, and Montana-raised steaks. The chalet's terrace is an ideal spot for a romantic dinner, with views of the surrounding mountains.

Picnic Spots

For those who prefer to dine al fresco, Glacier National Park offers numerous picnic spots where you can enjoy your meal surrounded by nature. These areas are perfect for families, hikers, or anyone looking to take a break in the midst of their adventures.

1. **Apgar Picnic Area**
   - **Location**: Near Apgar Village, West Glacier
   - **Details**: Located along the shores of Lake McDonald, Apgar Picnic Area offers stunning lake views and easy access to nearby trails. Picnic tables are available, and the area is equipped with fire pits and grills. It's a great spot to relax after exploring the west side of the park.

2. **Logan Pass Picnic Area**
   - **Location**: Logan Pass Visitor Center
   - **Details**: At an elevation of 6,646 feet, Logan Pass is the highest point on the Going-to-the-Sun Road. The picnic area here offers breathtaking views of the surrounding peaks and wildflower meadows. It's an excellent location to enjoy a meal while taking in the dramatic scenery.

3. **Two Medicine Picnic Area**
   - **Location**: Two Medicine Lake
   - **Details**: This picnic area offers a peaceful setting along the shores of Two Medicine Lake. It's a quieter spot compared to some of the more popular areas of the park, making it ideal for a tranquil meal with views of the surrounding mountains and the lake's crystal-clear waters.

4. **St. Mary Picnic Area**
   - **Location**: St. Mary Lake

- **Details**: Located near the eastern entrance of the park, the St. Mary Picnic Area provides stunning views of St. Mary Lake and the nearby peaks. The area is equipped with picnic tables and grills, making it a great spot for a relaxing lunch after exploring the nearby trails.

Grocery Stores and Supplies

Whether you're planning a picnic or stocking up for a backcountry adventure, several grocery stores and general stores within and around Glacier National Park offer everything you need.

1. **Apgar Village Market**
   - **Location**: Apgar Village, West Glacier
   - **Pricing**: Moderate
   - **Details**: This small market in Apgar Village offers a range of groceries, snacks, and beverages, along with camping supplies and souvenirs. It's a convenient stop for visitors staying in the Lake McDonald area or passing through on the Going-to-the-Sun Road.

2. **Swiftcurrent General Store**
   - **Location**: Many Glacier Valley
   - **Pricing**: Moderate
   - **Details**: Located in the heart of the Many Glacier area, this general store offers groceries, camping supplies, and a selection of sandwiches and snacks. It's a great place to grab supplies before heading out on a hike or stocking up for a day of exploration.

3. **Rising Sun Motor Inn and Campground Store**
   - **Location**: Rising Sun, St. Mary
   - **Pricing**: Moderate
   - **Details**: This store offers a range of groceries, snacks, and camping supplies, as well as a small selection of souvenirs. It's conveniently located

near the St. Mary entrance, making it a good stop for those entering the park from the east.

4. **Glacier Park Trading Co.**
   - **Location**: East Glacier Park Village
   - **Pricing**: Moderate
   - **Details**: Just outside the park's east entrance, this general store offers groceries, camping supplies, and a deli counter with sandwiches and snacks. It's a convenient stop for visitors staying in the East Glacier area or heading into the park from the east.

Local Cuisine and Must-Try Dishes

While Glacier National Park is known for its natural beauty, the local cuisine is also worth exploring. The park and its surrounding areas offer a taste of Montana's culinary traditions, with an emphasis on local ingredients and flavors.

1. **Huckleberries**

   ○ **Details**: Huckleberries are a local delicacy in Montana, and you'll find them featured in many dishes around the park. From huckleberry pancakes and pies to jams and sauces, this sweet and tart berry is a must-try during your visit.

2. **Bison**

   ○ **Details**: Bison is a staple of Montana cuisine, and many of the park's restaurants offer dishes featuring this lean and flavorful meat. Try a bison burger at Two Dog Flats Grill or bison meatloaf at Lake McDonald Lodge for a true taste of the region.

3. **Montana Trout**

- **Details**: Freshwater trout is another popular dish in Glacier National Park. Whether grilled, smoked, or pan-fried, it's often served with locally sourced vegetables and herbs. The Ptarmigan Dining Room at Many Glacier Hotel offers a particularly excellent trout dish.

4. **Huckleberry Ice Cream**
    - **Details**: No visit to Glacier National Park would be complete without trying huckleberry ice cream. This sweet treat is available at several locations within the park, including the shops in Apgar Village and the Many Glacier Hotel.

Souvenir Shops and Artisans

Bringing home a piece of Glacier National Park is a great way to remember your trip. The park and its surrounding communities offer a variety of shops where you can find everything from traditional souvenirs to locally made crafts and artwork.

1. **Glacier National Park Conservancy Stores**
    - **Location**: Multiple locations, including Apgar Visitor Center and Logan Pass Visitor Center
    - **Details**: Operated by the Glacier National Park Conservancy, these stores offer a range of park-themed merchandise, including clothing, books, maps, and educational materials. Proceeds from sales support the park's preservation efforts.
2. **Cedar Tree Gift Shop**
    - **Location**: Lake McDonald Lodge
    - **Details**: Located inside the historic Lake McDonald Lodge, this gift shop offers a selection of souvenirs, including clothing, jewelry, and home decor items. The shop also features locally made huckleberry products, perfect for taking home a taste of Montana.
3. **Many Glacier Hotel Gift Shop**
    - **Location**: Many Glacier Hotel
    - **Details**: The gift shop at Many Glacier Hotel offers a variety of souvenirs, including clothing, books, and handcrafted items from local artisans. You'll also find a selection of Native American crafts and jewelry, making it a great place to find unique and meaningful gifts.
4. **The Glacier Trading Post**
    - **Location**: St. Mary

○ **Details**: Just outside the park's east entrance, the Glacier Trading Post offers a wide range of souvenirs, including T-shirts, hats, and mugs, as well as a selection of Native American crafts and huckleberry products.

5. **West Glacier Gift Shop**
   ○ **Location**: West Glacier Village
   ○ **Details**: This shop offers a variety of Glacier National Park-themed merchandise, including clothing, accessories, and home decor items. It's a great stop for those looking to pick up souvenirs before leaving the park.

Artisans and Local Crafts

Montana is home to a thriving community of artisans, many of whom are inspired by the natural beauty of Glacier National Park. From handcrafted jewelry to pottery and paintings, you'll find a wide range of locally made items that reflect the spirit of the region.

1. **Great Northern Railway Framed Prints**
   ○ **Location**: Available at various gift shops within the park
   ○ **Details**: These vintage-style prints feature iconic scenes from Glacier National Park, inspired by the Great Northern Railway's historic advertising campaigns. They make a perfect souvenir for history buffs and art lovers alike.
2. **Native American Crafts**
   ○ **Location**: Many Glacier Hotel Gift Shop, St. Mary Visitor Center
   ○ **Details**: The Blackfeet, Salish, Kootenai, and Pend d'Oreille tribes have deep connections to the land that is now Glacier National Park. You can find a variety of Native American crafts and jewelry, including beadwork, pottery, and traditional art, at gift shops throughout the park.
3. **Handcrafted Huckleberry Products**
   ○ **Location**: Various shops in and around the park
   ○ **Details**: Huckleberries are a quintessential part of the Glacier experience, and you'll find a variety of handcrafted huckleberry products available for purchase. From jams and syrups to chocolates and teas, these make for delicious and unique gifts.
4. **Local Pottery and Ceramics**
   ○ **Location**: Available at select gift shops and artisan markets in West Glacier and St. Mary

- ○ **Details**: Montana's artisans create beautiful pottery and ceramics inspired by the natural beauty of the region. Look for pieces that incorporate local materials and designs, such as mountain landscapes and wildlife motifs.

5. **Handmade Jewelry**
   - ○ **Location**: Available at gift shops in Apgar Village, Lake McDonald Lodge, and Many Glacier Hotel
   - ○ **Details**: Montana is known for its gemstones, including sapphires and agates. Many local artisans create beautiful handmade jewelry featuring these stones, along with designs inspired by the park's rugged landscapes.

Day Trips and Nearby Attractions

Glacier National Park offers more than just breathtaking vistas and outdoor adventures within its boundaries. The surrounding areas are rich with opportunities for exploration, from charming towns and vast wilderness areas to stunning cross-border parks. Whether you're looking to experience more of Montana's natural beauty or explore nearby communities, this chapter highlights some of the best day trips and nearby attractions, complete with locations and pricing information.

Exploring the Flathead Valley

The Flathead Valley, located just outside Glacier National Park, is a region filled with natural wonders, outdoor activities, and small-town charm. This area is a gateway to many of Montana's most treasured landscapes and offers a diverse array of experiences for visitors.

1. **Flathead Lake**
   - **Location**: 35 miles south of Kalispell
   - **Activities**: Boating, fishing, swimming, hiking

- o **Pricing**: Free entry; boat rentals start at $50 per hour
- o **Details**: Flathead Lake is the largest natural freshwater lake west of the Mississippi, spanning nearly 200 square miles. The lake's crystal-clear waters are ideal for boating, fishing, and swimming. Multiple state parks around the lake, such as Big Arm State Park and Finley Point, offer picnic areas, hiking trails, and camping facilities. Visitors can rent boats or kayaks from local marinas, with prices starting at around $50 per hour for a small motorboat.

2. **Bigfork**
   - o **Location**: 20 miles southeast of Kalispell
   - o **Activities**: Art galleries, boutique shopping, dining
   - o **Pricing**: Free to explore; dining costs range from $15 to $40 per person
   - o **Details**: Nestled on the northeast shore of Flathead Lake, Bigfork is a picturesque village known for its vibrant arts scene and charming downtown area. The town is home to numerous art galleries, unique shops, and fine dining restaurants. Bigfork's quaint streets are perfect for a leisurely stroll, and the village often hosts art festivals and live performances during the summer months. Dining options range from casual eateries like Flathead Lake Brewing Co. to upscale restaurants such as The Raven, where you can enjoy locally sourced dishes with stunning lake views.

3. **Flathead National Forest**
   - o **Location**: Surrounds the Flathead Valley
   - o **Activities**: Hiking, wildlife viewing, camping
   - o **Pricing**: Free entry; campground fees range from $15 to $30 per night
   - o **Details**: Encompassing over 2.4 million acres, Flathead National Forest offers endless opportunities for outdoor adventure. The forest is home to hundreds of miles of hiking trails, ranging from easy strolls to challenging backcountry routes. Popular trails include the Jewel Basin Hiking Area, known for its alpine lakes and panoramic views, and the Holland Falls National Recreation Trail, which leads to a stunning waterfall. Camping is available at several campgrounds throughout the forest, with fees typically ranging from $15 to $30 per night.

Whitefish: A Gateway to Glacier

Whitefish, located just 25 miles west of Glacier National Park, is a charming town that serves as a popular base for exploring the park and the surrounding region. Known for its vibrant downtown, outdoor activities, and welcoming atmosphere, Whitefish is a must-visit destination in its own right.

1. **Whitefish Mountain Resort**
   - **Location**: 8 miles north of Whitefish
   - **Activities**: Skiing, snowboarding, hiking, mountain biking
   - **Pricing**: Lift tickets range from $60 to $90; summer activities start at $20
   - **Details**: Whitefish Mountain Resort is a year-round destination, offering world-class skiing and snowboarding in the winter and a wide range of summer activities, including hiking, mountain biking, and zip-lining. The resort boasts over 3,000 acres of skiable terrain and more than 300 inches of annual snowfall, making it a paradise for winter sports enthusiasts. In the summer, visitors can take advantage of the resort's extensive trail system, enjoy scenic chairlift rides, or try their hand at the resort's zip-line tours, with prices starting at $20 per person.

2. **Downtown Whitefish**
   - **Location**: Central Whitefish
   - **Activities**: Shopping, dining, entertainment
   - **Pricing**: Free to explore; dining costs range from $10 to $50 per person

- **Details**: Downtown Whitefish is a bustling hub of activity, offering a mix of boutique shops, art galleries, and restaurants. The town's laid-back vibe and friendly atmosphere make it a great place to spend an afternoon. Popular dining spots include Tupelo Grille, known for its Cajun-inspired dishes, and Loula's Café, a local favorite for breakfast and brunch. In the evenings, downtown Whitefish comes alive with live music, theater performances, and events at venues like the O'Shaughnessy Center.

3. **Whitefish Lake State Park**
   - **Location**: 3 miles west of downtown Whitefish
   - **Activities**: Swimming, boating, fishing, picnicking
   - **Pricing**: Day-use fee of $8 per vehicle
   - **Details**: Located just a short drive from downtown, Whitefish Lake State Park offers a beautiful setting for a variety of outdoor activities. The park features a sandy beach, boat launch, and picnic areas, making it a popular spot for swimming, boating, and fishing. Kayaks, canoes, and paddleboards are available for rent at the park, and the calm waters of Whitefish Lake are perfect for a relaxing day on the water.

Waterton Lakes National Park (Canada)

Waterton Lakes National Park, located just across the Canadian border, is the sister park to Glacier National Park and part of the Waterton-Glacier International Peace Park. This UNESCO World Heritage Site offers stunning landscapes, diverse wildlife, and a unique blend of natural beauty and cultural heritage.

1. **Waterton Village**
   - **Location**: Central Waterton Lakes National Park, Alberta, Canada
   - **Activities**: Dining, shopping, boat tours
   - **Pricing**: Entry fee of CAD $10 per person; boat tours start at CAD $50
   - **Details**: Waterton Village is the heart of Waterton Lakes National Park, offering a range of amenities, including restaurants, shops, and accommodations. The village is also the starting point for many of the park's activities, including boat tours on Upper Waterton Lake. These tours provide an opportunity to explore the park's stunning landscapes from the water and often include wildlife sightings. Dining options in the village range from casual cafés to fine dining, with prices typically ranging from CAD $15 to $50 per person.

2. **Red Rock Canyon**
   - **Location**: 10 miles from Waterton Village
   - **Activities**: Hiking, photography, wildlife viewing
   - **Pricing**: Included with park entry
   - **Details**: Red Rock Canyon is one of the most popular attractions in Waterton Lakes National Park, known for its striking red and green rock formations. The short, easy trail around the canyon offers spectacular views and is a great spot for photography. The area is also home to a variety of wildlife, including bighorn sheep and black bears, making it a popular destination for nature enthusiasts.

3. **Cameron Lake**
   - **Location**: 10 miles from Waterton Village
   - **Activities**: Boating, fishing, hiking
   - **Pricing**: Included with park entry; boat rentals start at CAD $20 per hour
   - **Details**: Nestled in a scenic valley, Cameron Lake is a beautiful spot for a day of relaxation and outdoor activities. The lake is surrounded by towering peaks and offers calm waters for boating and fishing. Canoes, kayaks, and paddleboats are available for rent, with prices starting at CAD $20 per hour. The area also features a picturesque hiking trail that follows the shoreline, offering stunning views of the lake and surrounding mountains.

North Fork Area and Polebridge

The North Fork area of Glacier National Park, including the tiny community of Polebridge, is one of the park's most remote and rugged regions. This area offers a unique experience for those looking to escape the crowds and explore the park's wild and untamed landscapes.

1. **Polebridge Mercantile**
    - **Location**: Polebridge, Montana
    - **Activities**: Shopping, dining
    - **Pricing**: Pastries range from $3 to $7; souvenirs from $5 to $50
    - **Details**: The Polebridge Mercantile is a historic general store that has been serving visitors and locals for over a century. Famous for its freshly baked pastries, including huckleberry bear claws and cinnamon rolls, the Mercantile is a must-visit for anyone exploring the North Fork area. The store also offers a selection of souvenirs, local crafts, and basic supplies. Prices for pastries range from $3 to $7, while souvenirs vary from $5 to $50.

2. **Bowman Lake**
    - **Location**: 6 miles from Polebridge
    - **Activities**: Hiking, fishing, kayaking
    - **Pricing**: Free entry; camping fees start at $15 per night

- **Details**: Bowman Lake is one of the most serene and picturesque spots in Glacier National Park. The lake is surrounded by dense forests and towering peaks, offering a peaceful retreat for those looking to connect with nature. The area offers several hiking trails, including the Bowman Lake Trail, which follows the shoreline and provides stunning views of the lake and surrounding wilderness. Fishing and kayaking are also popular activities at Bowman Lake, and the nearby campground offers a quiet place to spend the night, with fees starting at $15 per night.

3. **Kintla Lake**
   - **Location**: 15 miles from Polebridge
   - **Activities**: Camping, hiking, fishing
   - **Pricing**: Free entry; camping fees start at $15 per night
   - **Details**: Kintla Lake, located further up the North Fork, is even more remote and less visited than Bowman Lake. This pristine lake offers a true backcountry experience, with limited facilities and a focus on wilderness preservation. The Kintla Lake Campground is a primitive site, offering basic amenities for those looking to camp in a remote setting. The lake is popular for fishing, and the surrounding area offers excellent opportunities for hiking and wildlife viewing.

1. **Chinese Wall**
   - **Location**: Central Bob Marshall Wilderness
   - **Activities**: Backpacking, photography, wildlife viewing
   - **Pricing**: Free entry
   - **Details**: The Chinese Wall is one of the most iconic features of the Bob Marshall Wilderness. This massive limestone escarpment stretches for over 12 miles and rises nearly 1,000 feet above the surrounding landscape. Reaching the Chinese Wall requires a multi-day backpacking trip, but the effort is well worth it for the unparalleled views and sense of solitude. Along the way, you may encounter wildlife such as grizzly bears, elk, and mountain goats.

2. **South Fork Flathead River**
   - **Location**: Flows through the Bob Marshall Wilderness
   - **Activities**: Fishing, rafting, camping
   - **Pricing**: Free entry; guided trips start at $200 per person
   - **Details**: The South Fork Flathead River is a pristine waterway that flows through the heart of the Bob Marshall Wilderness. The river is renowned for its fly fishing, with anglers coming from around the world to catch

native cutthroat trout. The river is also popular for rafting, offering both serene stretches and more challenging rapids. Guided fishing and rafting trips are available, with prices starting at around $200 per person for a full-day excursion.

Kalispell and Other Nearby Towns

Kalispell, the largest town in the Flathead Valley, serves as the commercial and cultural hub of the region. Along with nearby towns like Columbia Falls and Hungry Horse, Kalispell offers a range of attractions, from historical sites and museums to shopping and dining.

1. **Conrad Mansion Museum**
   - **Location**: 330 Woodland Ave, Kalispell, Montana
   - **Activities**: Historical tours, events
   - **Pricing**: Admission is $15 for adults, $6 for children
   - **Details**: The Conrad Mansion Museum is a beautifully preserved example of Victorian architecture, offering a glimpse into the life of one of Kalispell's founding families. The mansion features original furnishings and artifacts from the early 1900s, and guided tours provide fascinating insights into the history of the area. The museum also hosts special events throughout the year, including tea parties and holiday tours.

2. **Hockaday Museum of Art**
   - **Location**: 302 2nd Ave E, Kalispell, Montana
   - **Activities**: Art exhibits, educational programs
   - **Pricing**: Admission is $10 for adults, $4 for children
   - **Details**: The Hockaday Museum of Art is dedicated to preserving and promoting the art and culture of Montana. The museum's collection includes works by prominent Montana artists, as well as Native American art and artifacts. In addition to its permanent collection, the museum hosts rotating exhibits and educational programs for visitors of all ages.

3. **Columbia Falls**
   - **Location**: 15 miles northeast of Kalispell
   - **Activities**: Shopping, dining, outdoor activities
   - **Pricing**: Free to explore; dining costs range from $10 to $30 per person
   - **Details**: Columbia Falls is a small town located just outside the west entrance of Glacier National Park. The town offers a variety of shops, restaurants, and outdoor activities, making it a convenient stop for visitors

to the park. Popular dining options include Three Forks Grille, which offers farm-to-table cuisine, and Nite Owl Restaurant, known for its hearty breakfasts and friendly service. Columbia Falls is also home to several outdoor outfitters, offering equipment rentals and guided tours for activities such as fishing, rafting, and horseback riding.

Suggested Itineraries for Glacier National Park

Glacier National Park offers a wide range of experiences, from breathtaking hikes and scenic drives to wildlife viewing and cultural exploration. Depending on the length of your stay and your interests, here are some suggested itineraries to help you make the most of your visit to this stunning national park.

1-Day Itinerary: Glacier's Highlights

Morning:

- **Going-to-the-Sun Road**: Start your day early by driving the Going-to-the-Sun Road, the park's most famous scenic drive. Begin at the West Glacier entrance and head east. Along the way, stop at the Lake McDonald Lodge for a quick look at this historic site and its stunning views of Lake McDonald.
- **Logan Pass Visitor Center**: Continue your drive up to Logan Pass, the highest point on the Going-to-the-Sun Road. Spend some time exploring the visitor center and take a short hike along the Hidden Lake Overlook Trail (2.7 miles round trip) for spectacular views of Hidden Lake and the surrounding peaks.

Afternoon:

- **St. Mary Lake and Wild Goose Island**: Continue east on the Going-to-the-Sun Road, stopping at the Wild Goose Island Overlook for a classic view of St. Mary Lake with its iconic island. This is one of the most photographed spots in the park.
- **St. Mary Visitor Center**: End your drive at the St. Mary Visitor Center, where you can learn more about the park's natural and cultural history. Enjoy a picnic lunch at the nearby St. Mary Picnic Area.

Evening:

- **Two Medicine Valley**: If time allows, head south to Two Medicine Valley, one of the park's quieter areas. Take a short hike along the Running Eagle Falls Trail (0.6 miles round trip) or simply enjoy the peaceful atmosphere of Two Medicine Lake.

2-Day Itinerary: A Deeper Dive into Glacier

Day 1:

Morning:

- **Going-to-the-Sun Road**: Start your journey on the Going-to-the-Sun Road as outlined in the 1-day itinerary. Take your time exploring the scenic viewpoints and hiking the Hidden Lake Overlook Trail at Logan Pass.

Afternoon:

- **Many Glacier Valley**: After lunch, drive to Many Glacier Valley, often referred to as the "Switzerland of North America." Take a boat tour on Swiftcurrent Lake and Lake Josephine, or hike the Grinnell Lake Trail (7.1 miles round trip) for stunning views of glaciers, lakes, and waterfalls.

Evening:

- **Many Glacier Hotel**: Spend the night at the historic Many Glacier Hotel. Enjoy dinner at the Ptarmigan Dining Room and unwind while taking in the views of Swiftcurrent Lake.

Day 2:

Morning:

- **Grinnell Glacier Hike**: For an adventurous start to your second day, hike the Grinnell Glacier Trail (10.3 miles round trip), one of the park's most popular hikes. The trail offers incredible views of Grinnell Glacier, turquoise lakes, and abundant wildlife. For a shorter option, take the boat shuttle across Swiftcurrent Lake and Lake Josephine, which cuts off 3.4 miles from the hike.

Afternoon:

- **Iceberg Lake Hike**: If you're up for more hiking, tackle the Iceberg Lake Trail (9.7 miles round trip), which leads to a stunning glacial lake often dotted with floating icebergs. Alternatively, explore the trails around Many Glacier Valley, such as the Swiftcurrent Pass Trail.

Evening:

- **Return to St. Mary or West Glacier**: Depending on your lodging, return to St. Mary or West Glacier for the night. Consider dining at a local restaurant such as the Snowgoose Grille in St. Mary.

3-Day Itinerary: Comprehensive Glacier Experience

Day 1:

- **Follow the 1-Day Itinerary**: Begin your adventure with the 1-day itinerary, taking in the highlights along the Going-to-the-Sun Road and exploring Logan Pass and St. Mary Lake.

Day 2:

- **Many Glacier Valley**: Dive into the Many Glacier area as described in the 2-day itinerary. Enjoy the Grinnell Glacier Hike, boat tours, or other trails in the valley. Stay overnight at Many Glacier Hotel or a nearby campground.

Day 3:

Morning:

- **Two Medicine Valley**: Head to Two Medicine Valley in the morning. Take the boat tour on Two Medicine Lake and hike to Twin Falls (3.8 miles round trip) or simply enjoy the serene views of the surrounding peaks.

Afternoon:

- **North Fork and Polebridge**: Drive to the remote North Fork area and visit the rustic Polebridge Mercantile for a delicious huckleberry pastry. Explore the Bowman Lake area, where you can hike or simply relax by the peaceful lakeshore.

Evening:

- **Sunset at Lake McDonald**: On your way back to West Glacier, stop at Lake McDonald to catch the sunset. The calm waters and colorful sky create a picture-perfect ending to your Glacier National Park adventure.

5-Day Itinerary: In-Depth Glacier Exploration

Day 1:

- **Going-to-the-Sun Road**: Follow the 1-day itinerary, taking your time to explore each stop and hike at Logan Pass. Spend the night in West Glacier or St. Mary.

Day 2:

- **Many Glacier Valley**: Spend the entire day in Many Glacier Valley, enjoying a mix of hiking, boat tours, and wildlife watching. Stay overnight at Many Glacier Hotel or a nearby campsite.

Day 3:

- **Two Medicine Valley**: Explore Two Medicine as described in the 3-day itinerary. Stay overnight at the Two Medicine Campground or return to St. Mary.

Day 4:

Morning:

- **Waterton Lakes National Park (Canada)**: Cross the border into Canada and visit Waterton Lakes National Park. Spend the morning exploring Waterton Village and taking a boat tour on Upper Waterton Lake.

Afternoon:

- **Red Rock Canyon and Cameron Lake**: Spend the afternoon visiting Red Rock Canyon and Cameron Lake, two of Waterton's most scenic spots. Return to Glacier National Park in the evening, staying in St. Mary or Many Glacier.

Day 5:

Morning:

- **North Fork and Polebridge**: Visit the remote North Fork area and Polebridge, as described in the 3-day itinerary. Enjoy the rugged beauty of Bowman Lake or Kintla Lake.

Afternoon:

- **Kalispell or Whitefish**: On your way back, stop in Kalispell or Whitefish for a taste of local culture. Explore the shops, galleries, and restaurants before heading back to your lodging in West Glacier or Whitefish.

Evening:

- **Final Night at Glacier**: Enjoy a relaxing evening reflecting on your Glacier National Park adventure, perhaps with a meal at a local restaurant or a quiet evening by the lake.

7-Day Itinerary: Ultimate Glacier and Beyond Adventure

Day 1:

- **Going-to-the-Sun Road**: Kick off your trip with a thorough exploration of the Going-to-the-Sun Road, hiking at Logan Pass and enjoying the scenic overlooks. Spend the night in West Glacier or St. Mary.

Day 2:

- **Many Glacier Valley**: Immerse yourself in the beauty of Many Glacier, hiking to Grinnell Glacier or taking a boat tour. Spend the night in Many Glacier.

Day 3:

- **Two Medicine Valley**: Spend a full day in Two Medicine, hiking, boating, and exploring. Consider camping at the Two Medicine Campground.

Day 4:

- **Waterton Lakes National Park (Canada)**: Cross the border and explore Waterton Lakes National Park, including Waterton Village, Red Rock Canyon, and Cameron Lake. Stay overnight in Waterton or return to Glacier.

Day 5:

- **North Fork and Polebridge**: Head to the remote North Fork area, visiting Polebridge Mercantile and exploring Bowman or Kintla Lake. Stay overnight in a rustic cabin or camp in the area.

Day 6:

Morning:

- **The Bob Marshall Wilderness**: Spend the day exploring the edges of The Bob Marshall Wilderness Complex, perhaps hiking or fishing near the South Fork Flathead River or visiting the Spotted Bear Ranger Station.

Afternoon:

- **Flathead Lake**: On your way back, visit Flathead Lake for a relaxing afternoon of boating, swimming, or simply enjoying the views. Stay overnight in Kalispell or Bigfork.

Day 7:

Morning:

- **Whitefish**: Spend your final day exploring Whitefish, visiting Whitefish Mountain Resort, downtown shops, and enjoying a meal at a local restaurant.

Afternoon:

- **Final Drive**: Take a leisurely drive back to your starting point, reflecting on the incredible experiences and scenery you've encountered throughout your trip.

Evening:

- **Departure**: End your Glacier National Park adventure with a final sunset, whether at Lake McDonald or Whitefish Lake, before departing for your next destination.

ITINERARY PLANNER

FLIGHT DETAILS

DETAILS	DEPARTURE FLIGHT	RETURN FLIGHT
DATE		
FROM		
DEPARTURE TIME		
TO		
ARRIVAL TIME		
FLIGHT		
AIRLINE		

LODGING

LOCATION:

ADDRESS:

PHONE:

ACTIVITIES

DATE	TIME	LOCATION	ACTIVITY

Travel Resources

When planning a visit to Glacier National Park, having the right resources at your disposal can significantly enhance your experience. Whether you're navigating the park's vast trail system, seeking the best places to stay and eat, or ensuring your safety, being well-prepared with maps, guides, apps, and contacts is essential. This chapter provides a comprehensive overview of the travel resources you'll need, from practical tools like park maps and trail guides to critical information such as local emergency contacts.

Park Maps and Trail Guides

Navigating Glacier National Park's expansive and rugged landscape requires reliable maps and trail guides. These resources are indispensable for planning hikes, finding scenic drives, and discovering the park's hidden gems.

1. Official Glacier National Park Map

- **Availability:** Provided at park entrances and visitor centers; downloadable from the National Park Service (NPS) website
- **Cost:** Free

The official Glacier National Park map is your most essential tool for exploring the park. It highlights all major roads, trailheads, campgrounds, visitor centers, and points of interest. The map is color-coded to indicate different types of terrain, making it easier to plan your routes and identify areas of interest. The map also includes information on park regulations, safety tips, and services available within the park.

Key Points:

- **Essential Navigation:** The map provides a comprehensive overview of the park, helping visitors navigate its vast and complex terrain.

- **Accessibility:** The map is readily available at multiple locations within the park and online, ensuring you can access it before and during your visit.

2. Detailed Trail Guides

- **Availability:** Available at visitor centers, outdoor shops in nearby towns, and online retailers like Amazon
- **Cost:** $10 to $25, depending on the guide

Trail guides offer detailed descriptions of Glacier National Park's extensive trail network. These guides typically include information on trail difficulty, length, elevation gain, and points of interest along the way. Some popular guides also feature topographic maps, GPS coordinates, and tips for wildlife viewing. They are invaluable for hikers looking to explore the park's backcountry or less-traveled paths.

Key Points:

- **Comprehensive Information:** Trail guides provide in-depth details about specific hikes, helping you choose trails that match your skill level and interests.
- **Safety and Preparation:** These guides often include safety tips and advice on what to pack, ensuring you're well-prepared for your hikes.

3. Topographic Maps

- **Availability:** Available at visitor centers, outdoor retailers, and online
- **Cost:** $10 to $15 per map

Topographic maps are essential for serious hikers and backcountry adventurers. These maps provide detailed information on the park's terrain, including contour lines, elevations, and natural features such as rivers, lakes, and glaciers. Topographic maps are particularly useful for planning off-trail routes or navigating remote areas where the landscape can be challenging.

Key Points:

- **Detailed Terrain Information:** Topographic maps offer a detailed view of the park's geography, making them essential for backcountry exploration.
- **Safety Tool:** In areas without cell service or GPS signal, a topographic map can be a crucial tool for navigation and safety.

Essential Apps and Websites

In the digital age, mobile apps and websites have become vital tools for travelers. Glacier National Park visitors can benefit from a variety of apps and websites that provide real-time information, navigation assistance, and trip-planning resources.

1. Glacier National Park App

- **Availability:** Available for download on iOS and Android devices
- **Cost:** Free

The official Glacier National Park app, developed by the National Park Service, is an all-in-one resource for park visitors. The app features interactive maps, trail information, and real-time updates on road conditions, weather, and park alerts. It also includes a GPS-enabled trail map that can be used offline, making it a valuable tool even in areas without cell service.

Key Points:

- **Real-Time Information:** The app provides up-to-date information on road closures, weather conditions, and more, helping you plan your day effectively.
- **Offline Access:** The offline map feature ensures you can navigate the park even when you're out of range of a cell signal.

2. AllTrails

- **Availability:** Available for download on iOS and Android devices; also accessible via web browser
- **Cost:** Free version available; premium subscription costs $29.99 per year

AllTrails is a popular app and website that offers detailed information on thousands of trails worldwide, including many in Glacier National Park. The app includes user reviews, trail maps, difficulty ratings, and GPS tracking features. AllTrails is particularly useful for finding lesser-known hikes and reading about other hikers' experiences.

Key Points:

- **User-Generated Content:** AllTrails provides insights from fellow hikers, including reviews, photos, and trail conditions.

- **Navigation Tools:** The GPS tracking feature helps you stay on course, and the app's maps can be downloaded for offline use.

3. NPS.gov/Glacier

- **Availability:** Accessible via any web browser
- **Cost:** Free

The official Glacier National Park website, managed by the National Park Service, is a comprehensive resource for planning your trip. The site includes information on park hours, entrance fees, camping reservations, road conditions, and more. It's an excellent starting point for anyone planning a visit to the park.

Key Points:

- **Comprehensive Resource:** The website covers everything from basic park information to detailed guides on specific activities and locations.
- **Current Conditions:** Regularly updated with current conditions and alerts, ensuring you have the latest information before your visit.

4. Recreation.gov

- **Availability:** Accessible via any web browser and as a mobile app on iOS and Android
- **Cost:** Free to use; reservation fees vary depending on the activity

Recreation.gov is the official platform for booking campsites, backcountry permits, and ranger-led activities in Glacier National Park. The website and app allow you to search for available campsites, view site details, and make reservations. It also provides information on availability and booking for popular activities like boat tours and guided hikes.

Key Points:

- **Reservation System:** Essential for securing campsites and permits, especially during peak season when demand is high.
- **User-Friendly Interface:** The platform makes it easy to search for and book various recreational activities within the park.

Local Emergency Contacts

Safety is a top priority when exploring Glacier National Park, and it's essential to be prepared for any emergencies. Having a list of local emergency contacts can make a significant difference in case of an accident, medical emergency, or other urgent situation.

1. Park Rangers and Emergency Services

- **Contact Number:** 911 for emergencies; (406) 888-7800 for non-emergency assistance
- **Availability:** 24/7 emergency services; park rangers available during park operating hours

In case of an emergency, calling 911 will connect you to local emergency services, including search and rescue teams. For non-emergency situations, such as reporting lost items or seeking advice on safety concerns, you can contact park rangers at the park's main information number.

Key Points:

- **Emergency Response:** Park rangers are trained to handle a variety of emergencies, from medical incidents to lost hikers.
- **Rapid Assistance:** Knowing the emergency contact number ensures you can quickly reach help if needed.

2. Local Hospitals and Medical Facilities

- **Kalispell Regional Medical Center**
  - **Location:** 310 Sunnyview Lane, Kalispell, MT
  - **Contact:** (406) 752-5111
  - **Distance:** Approximately 30 miles from West Glacier
- **North Valley Hospital**
  - **Location:** 1600 Hospital Way, Whitefish, MT
  - **Contact:** (406) 863-3500
  - **Distance:** Approximately 40 miles from West Glacier

In the event of a medical emergency that requires more than first aid, the nearest hospitals are in Kalispell and Whitefish. Both facilities offer full medical services, including emergency care.

Key Points:

- **Proximity:** Kalispell and Whitefish are the closest towns with full-service hospitals, making them the go-to options for medical emergencies.
- **Comprehensive Care:** These hospitals provide a wide range of medical services, ensuring you can receive appropriate care for any condition.

3. Local Law Enforcement

- **Glacier National Park Law Enforcement**
  - **Contact Number:** (406) 888-7801 (for non-emergencies)
- **Flathead County Sheriff's Office**
  - **Location:** 920 South Main Street, Kalispell, MT
  - **Contact:** (406) 758-5585

The park's law enforcement rangers and the Flathead County Sheriff's Office handle law enforcement within and around Glacier National Park. For non-emergency law enforcement issues, such as reporting suspicious activity or lost property, you can contact these agencies directly.

Key Points:

- **Law Enforcement Support:** The park's rangers and local sheriff's office are available to assist with law enforcement issues within the park and surrounding areas.
- **Quick Access:** Having these contact numbers on hand ensures you can report any issues promptly.

Visitor Centers and Information

Glacier National Park's visitor centers are invaluable resources for anyone exploring the park. They provide maps, guides, educational exhibits, and advice from knowledgeable rangers.

1. Apgar Visitor Center

- **Location:** Near the West Glacier Entrance
- **Hours:** Typically open daily from 8:00 AM to 5:00 PM during peak season
- **Pricing:** Free with park admission

Apgar Visitor Center is the main visitor center on the west side of the park. It offers a wealth of resources, including detailed maps, trail guides, and exhibits on the park's natural and cultural history. Rangers are available to answer questions, provide safety tips, and offer recommendations on the best activities and routes based on current conditions. The center also serves as a hub for ranger-led programs and the Native America Speaks presentations.

Key Points:

- **Comprehensive Information:** Apgar Visitor Center is an excellent first stop for visitors entering the park from the west, offering everything you need to plan your visit.
- **Ranger Assistance:** The rangers at Apgar are incredibly knowledgeable and can help tailor your visit to suit your interests and abilities.

2. Logan Pass Visitor Center

- **Location:** At the highest point of the Going-to-the-Sun Road
- **Hours:** Open daily during peak season, typically from 9:00 AM to 5:00 PM
- **Pricing:** Free with park admission

Logan Pass Visitor Center is located at one of the most popular and scenic spots in the park. The center provides information about the unique alpine environment of Logan Pass, including exhibits on local flora, fauna, and the effects of climate change on the park's glaciers. Rangers at Logan Pass also lead guided hikes and are available to answer questions about the area's trails and wildlife.

Key Points:

- **Scenic Location:** The visitor center offers breathtaking views and easy access to popular trails like the Hidden Lake Trail and the Highline Trail.
- **Educational Exhibits:** The exhibits provide valuable context for understanding the park's unique high-altitude ecosystem.

3. St. Mary Visitor Center

- **Location:** Near the St. Mary Entrance on the east side of the park
- **Hours:** Open daily from 8:00 AM to 5:00 PM during peak season
- **Pricing:** Free with park admission

St. Mary Visitor Center is the primary visitor center on the east side of Glacier National Park. It features exhibits on the park's geology, Native American history, and the impact of the Great Northern Railway. The center is also a starting point for many ranger-led activities and provides information on hiking trails, camping, and weather conditions on the east side of the park.

Key Points:

- **Eastern Gateway:** St. Mary is an important resource for visitors exploring the eastern regions of the park, including the Many Glacier and Two Medicine areas.
- **Cultural Exhibits:** The visitor center highlights the cultural history of the area, particularly the significance of the land to the Blackfeet Nation.

Final Tips for a Memorable Visit:

- **Plan Ahead:** Make reservations for lodging, camping, and popular activities well in advance, especially during peak season.
- **Stay Informed:** Regularly check the National Park Service website or app for updates on trail conditions, road closures, and weather forecasts.
- **Pack Accordingly:** Prepare for variable weather, bring necessary gear for hiking and camping, and always carry water and snacks.
- **Respect the Park:** Follow Leave No Trace principles, respect wildlife, and be mindful of park regulations to help preserve Glacier National Park for future generations.

Looking Ahead: Future of Glacier National Park

As we look to the future, Glacier National Park faces significant challenges, including the effects of climate change, increasing visitor numbers, and the need to balance conservation with recreation. The park's iconic glaciers are retreating, and the ecosystems are changing, which underscores the importance of ongoing conservation efforts.

- **Encouraging Stewardship and Conservation:** Every visitor to Glacier National Park has a role to play in its preservation. By following park rules, supporting sustainable tourism practices, and participating in educational programs, you can contribute to the park's long-term health. Consider supporting organizations that work to protect the park and its wildlife, and take the time to educate others about the importance of conserving this natural treasure.
- **Adapting to Change:** The future of Glacier National Park will likely involve adapting to new challenges. This may include changes in how the park is managed, how visitors are educated, and how the environment is protected. Staying informed and involved in these efforts is one way to ensure that Glacier remains a cherished destination for generations to come.

Made in the USA
Monee, IL
23 January 2025

10701096R00083